The Induction of Early Childhood Educators

Also Available from Bloomsbury

Digital Personalization in Early Childhood, Natalia Kucirkova
Digital Technologies in Early Childhood Art, Mona Sakr
The Early Childhood Educator, edited by Rachel Langford and Brooke Richardson
More-Than-Human Literacies in Early Childhood, Abigail Hackett
Pedagogical Leadership in Early Childhood Education, edited by Mona Sakr and June O'Sullivan
Social Leadership in Early Childhood Education and Care, June O'Sullivan and Mona Sakr
Issues and Challenges of Immigration in Early Childhood in the USA, Wilma Robles-Melendez and Wayne Driscoll
Qualitative Studies of Exploration in Childhood Education, edited by Marilyn Fleer, Mariane Hedegaard, Elin Eriksen Ødegaard and Hanne Værum Sørensen
Theorizing Feminist Ethics of Care in Early Childhood Practice, edited by Rachel Langford

The Induction of Early Childhood Educators

Retention, Needs, and Aspirations

Laura K. Doan

BLOOMSBURY ACADEMIC
LONDON • NEW YORK • OXFORD • NEW DELHI • SYDNEY

BLOOMSBURY ACADEMIC

Bloomsbury Publishing Plc, 50 Bedford Square, London, WC1B 3DP, UK
Bloomsbury Publishing Inc, 1359 Broadway, New York, NY 10018, USA
Bloomsbury Publishing Ireland, 29 Earlsfort Terrace, Dublin 2, D02 AY28, Ireland

BLOOMSBURY, BLOOMSBURY ACADEMIC and the Diana logo are trademarks of
Bloomsbury Publishing Plc

First published in Great Britain 2024
This paperback edition published in 2025

Copyright © Laura K. Doan, 2024

Laura K. Doan has asserted her right under the Copyright, Designs and Patents Act,
1988, to be identified as Author of this work.

For legal purposes the Acknowledgments on p. x constitute an extension
of this copyright page.

Cover image © Hugo Yuen

All rights reserved. No part of this publication may be: i) reproduced or transmitted
in any form, electronic or mechanical, including photocopying, recording or by means
of any information storage or retrieval system without prior permission in writing from the
publishers; or ii) used or reproduced in any way for the training, development or operation
of artificial intelligence (AI) technologies, including generative AI technologies. The rights
holders expressly reserve this publication from the text and data mining exception as
per Article 4(3) of the Digital Single Market Directive (EU) 2019/790.

Bloomsbury Publishing Plc does not have any control over, or responsibility for, any
third-party websites referred to or in this book. All internet addresses given in this
book were correct at the time of going to press. The author and publisher regret any
inconvenience caused if addresses have changed or sites have ceased to exist,
but can accept no responsibility for any such changes.

A catalogue record for this book is available from the British Library.

A catalog record for this book is available from the Library of Congress.

ISBN: HB: 978-1-3501-8722-1
PB: 978-1-3501-8745-0
ePDF: 978-1-3501-8723-8
eBook: 978-1-3501-8724-5

Typeset by Deanta Global Publishing Services, Chennai, India

For product safety related questions contact productsafety@bloomsbury.com.

To find out more about our authors and books visit www.bloomsbury.com and
sign up for our newsletters.

I dedicate this book to all early childhood educators. I see you. I hear you. I value you. Thank you for the incredible work you do to support young children and families in our neighborhoods, communities, and our society. I hope that this book will help to shed light onto your experiences as early childhood educators so that collectively we can ensure that you are supported fully.

Contents

List of Illustrations	viii
Preface	ix
Acknowledgments	x
Introduction	1
1 Theories and Practices Related to the Development of Educators	26
Part I Educators' Experiences in the First Five Years of Work	
2 The New Role	45
3 Adjusting to the Field of Early Childhood Education	62
4 Supervisory Practices	70
5 Induction Support	85
6 Key Themes	95
Part II Moving Forward	
7 Toward a Best Practice for Early Childhood Educators	109
8 Theories and New Directions in Early Childhood Education	125
Conclusion	142
References	145
Index	156

Illustrations

Figures

0.1	Issues facing novice early childhood educators	8
0.2	Theoretical framework	14
7.0	Model of how new educators are perceived	111
7.1	How beginning early childhood educators want to be treated	113
7.2	The isolated ECE workplace	115
7.3	The Doan model of best practice for the induction of beginning early childhood educators	118
8.0	What makes a Peer Mentoring Program successful	130
9.0	Life preserver	143

Tables

0.1	Introduction of Terms	3
0.2	Demographic Characteristics of Participants	17
2.0	Adjustment to Early Childhood Education Program Scale	46
2.1	Adjustment to New Role	47
3.0	Adjustment to Early Childhood Education Classroom Scale	63
3.1	Field of Early Childhood Education Scale	65
3.2	Teacher Job Satisfaction in Individual Items	68
4.0	Adjustment to Supervisory Practices	71
4.1	Adjustment to Administrative Practices	73
5.0	Percentage of Feedback, Observations, Professional Development, and Mentoring Received	86
5.1	Percentage of Other Induction Activities Received	88
5.2	Induction Activities	89
5.3	Rank Order of Scales Based on Level of Need	89

Preface

This book has been inspired by my desire to shed light onto the issues related to the retention of early childhood educators. In my work as an associate professor in an early childhood education post-secondary program, I have the privilege of seeing countless student educators who are passionate about their work with young children and families. Knowing that the passion is not enough to keep them in the field, I wondered what their experiences were, once they left the post-secondary system, and began working as an early childhood educator. I have focused on the ongoing professional identity development needs, the impact of educator efficacy, or an educator's confidence in their own ability, communities of practice, and peer mentoring. Not surprisingly, the educators themselves have great knowledge from their lived experiences as educators, and by joining with them, I have learned much about how best to support both beginning and experienced early childhood educators, so they can move from surviving to thriving.

Acknowledgments

I would like to offer my warmest thanks to the early childhood educators who have shared their stories, thoughts, and experiences with me. By doing so, you have helped to shed light on an under-researched area in early learning and care: the experiences of beginning early childhood educators.

I hope that all who read this book will be inspired by what is possible when we join with early childhood educators, giving educators a voice and full participation in both research and in designing programs of support for early childhood educators. Powerful things can happen when we work together.

Introduction

Overview of the Book

Politicians, educators, and policymakers across the world are recognizing the importance of early childhood education, and this has resulted in early learning frameworks being created in many countries across the world, including New Zealand (New Zealand Government, 2017), Australia (Government of Australia, 2018), Ireland (National Council for Curriculum and Assessment, 2009), and England (United Kingdom Government, 2021), for example. In Canada, where education is a provincial responsibility, early learning frameworks have been constructed in nine of the ten provinces, including Ontario (Government of Ontario, 2007), New Brunswick (Early Childhood Research and Development Team, 2011), Prince Edward Island (Flanagan, 2011), Alberta (Makovichuk et al., 2014), and British Columbia (Government of British Columbia, 2019). Decision-makers are recognizing the importance of quality early care and education of young children, realizing the "significant benefits to children, families, and society as a whole" (Lynch & Vaghul, 2015). One major factor in ensuring excellence in early childhood education programs is the quality of the staff, and knowledge of what helps beginning early childhood educators to become successfully inducted into the profession is an important part of ensuring quality early childhood education programs for children and families. This book shares information on the induction needs of beginning early childhood educators, those who have been working in the early childhood education field for five years or less, and is based on original research with beginning early childhood educators in British Columbia, Canada, conducted by me, the author. This is particularly important as there has been a gap in the literature on the subject of novice early childhood educators' needs (Neuman, Josephson, & Chua, 2015; Mahmood, 2012). This introduction begins with a definition of terms and an overview of the context and background for the book.

Definition of Terms

Terms and definitions have been provided to ensure a consistent understanding throughout the book (see Table 0.1). Care has been taken to include a range of definitions that includes both the context where the research took place (British Columbia, Canada) and international contexts.

Context

Qualifications of early childhood educators vary widely internationally, nationally, and provincially, with educators receiving a certificate, diploma, or degree in early childhood education. For example, in New Zealand, early childhood educators are involved in a two- to five-year process of induction and support prior to applying for "fully registered teacher status" (Aitken et al., 2008, p. 1). Early childhood educators are partially registered prior to concluding the induction process. In Canada, early childhood educators can be registered as assistants or as certified early childhood educators. Early childhood educators in British Columbia graduate with a certificate, which is completed in two semesters: a diploma, completed in three semesters; or a bachelor's degree, completed in four years. Bachelor's degrees in early childhood education are relatively new in British Columbia, and most early childhood educators graduate with a certificate or diploma. In addition to practica, early childhood educators are mandated by the province of British Columbia to complete 500 hours of paid or volunteer work in a licensed early childhood education program under the supervision of a certified educator. After completing their coursework and 500 hours of work experience, early childhood education graduates apply to the province to be certified, which is a requirement of early childhood practitioners who want to work in a licensed early childhood education program. This first license is valid for five years when the educator must go through a renewal process. The only requirement to renew one's license is to complete forty hours of professional development over the five-year time span (Government of British Columbia, 2022a).

Table 0.1 Introduction of Terms

Early Childhood Education and Care (ECE or ECEC)	"The period from birth to eight years old is one of remarkable brain development for children and represents a crucial window of opportunity for education. UNESCO believes early childhood care and education (ECCE) that is truly inclusive is much more than just preparation for primary school. It can be the foundation for emotional wellbeing and learning throughout life and one of the best investments a country can make as it promotes holistic development, gender equality and social cohesion" (UNESCO, 2022). Early childhood education is typically defined as, "programs and services for children from birth to age nine and their families" (Mayfield, 2001, p. 3). It includes day care, nursery school, kindergarten, and primary grades as well as other types of programs such as family support programs. In Australia, early learning programs include "long day care, occasional care, family day care, Multi-purpose Aboriginal Children's Services, preschools and kindergartens, playgroups, creches, early intervention settings and similar services" (Government of Australia, 2018, p. 8). In Finland, these are the core values of the curricula: The general principle of ECEC in Finland is that the best interest of the child shall always be the primary consideration. The child has a right to well-being, care, and protection, and his/her opinion is considered in decision-making. Equal and equitable treatment of all children as well as protection against discrimination are requirements, in accordance with the UN Convention on the Rights of the Child, the Act on Early Childhood Education and Care, and the UN Convention on the Rights of Persons with Disabilities. Underlying values in the national core curriculum for ECEC are: - Intrinsic value of childhood - Growth as a human being - Rights of the child - Equity, equality, and diversity - Diversity of families - Healthy and sustainable way of living. (Finnish National Agency for Education, 2022).

(*Continued*)

Table 0.1 (Continued)

Early Childhood Educators (ECEs):	In Canada, qualifications of early childhood educators vary. Currently, each province and territory is responsible for the delivery of early learning programs; however, recently all provinces and territories have signed agreements to move forward on a national child care program. In British Columbia: Early Childhood Educators (ECEs) specialize in the learning, development, and well-being of children from birth to five years old. ECEs are qualified to work in a variety of settings, including licensed child care facilities (Government of British Columbia, 2022b). Furthermore, early childhood educators: Have specialized post-secondary education and adhere to a Code of Ethics; Are certified through the provincial government; Consider children's developmental ages and stages in every facet of their work; Hold a core value of the importance of play in children's natural environment; and Work in provincially licensed and regulated community-based child care programs, preschools, Strong Start programs, and other related programs (Early Childhood Educators of British Columbia, 2009). Educators collaborate with children and their families as partners in research. This means educators are continually observing, listening, and experimenting with an openness to the unexpected. The role of the educator has shifted away from being a transmitter of knowledge toward being a collaborator who creates conditions so that children can invent, investigate, build theories, and learn. Educators work in relationship with children and strive to ensure children feel safe, confident, motivated, and listened to (Government of British Columbia, 2019, p. 16). Recently, the Early Childhood Educators of British Columbia (ECEBC) put forward a position paper on the role of the early childhood educator, which challenges dominant perspectives of the early childhood educator as a technician: The work of early childhood educators is "woven within diverse contexts, communities and settings. Inspired by the orientations of the BC Early Learning Framework, the early childhood educator in BC engages in pedagogical work with obligations and responsibilities necessary to move towards more livable worlds." This definition moves beyond the ECEBC Code of Ethics (2021) by "envisioning an early childhood educator who co-creates pedagogical spaces with children, families and communities. Through an ethics of care (Langford & Richardson, 2020), the early childhood educator holds a disposition to listen, to be open, to be challenged to think otherwise, to hold space for complexity, and to live joyfully" (Early Childhood Educators of British Columbia, 2022, pp. 2–3).

"ECEBC puts forward the following orientations that educators in BC engage with in pedagogical practices that envision more livable worlds:

Educators work with pedagogical commitments;
Educators respond to legacies of colonization;
Educators build responsive relationships;
Educators co-construct lively curriculum; and
Educators practice with ethical commitments" (ECEBC, 2022, pp. 3–5).

In the UK: the early framework is based on the following principles:

- every child is a unique child, who is constantly learning and can be resilient, capable, confident, and self-assured;
- children learn to be strong and independent through positive relationships;
- children learn and develop well in enabling environments with teaching and support from adults, who respond to their individual interests and needs and help them to build their learning over time. Children benefit from a strong partnership between practitioners and parents and/or carers;
- importance of learning and development. Children develop and learn at different rates;

Additionally, children are assigned a Key Person, who is responsible for ensuring that the child's individual needs, interests, and development are attended to (Department for Education, 2021).

In Australia:

"Children actively construct their own understandings and contribute to others' learning. They recognise their agency, capacity to initiate and lead learning, and their rights to participate in decisions that affect them, including their learning. Viewing children as active participants and decision makers opens up possibilities for educators to move beyond pre-conceived expectations about what children can do and learn. This requires educators to respect and work with each child's unique qualities and abilities. Educators' practices and the relationships they form with children and families have a significant effect on children's involvement and success in learning" (Government of Australia, 2018, p. 10).

In Finland, it is mandated "that at least one in every three educators in each day care center must be a kindergarten teacher who has a bachelor's degree in education (from a university), or a bachelor's degree in social sciences" (Salminen, 2017, p. 141).

(*Continued*)

Table 0.1 (Continued)

Early Childhood Education Instructor/Faculty Member/Professor/Lecturer:	A faculty member who teaches in a post-secondary early childhood education program.
Mentor Educator or Sponsor Educator:	A certified early childhood educator working in an early learning program who supports the student in their practicum by modeling skills, observing the student, and providing feedback (Doan, 2013). In New Zealand, early childhood teachers are provisionally registered and receive a mentor who is charged with supporting them in the process to becoming fully registered (Aitken et al., 2008).
Induction	Induction refers to both the time period when an early childhood educator is first in the field, usually the first year, and specific induction activities such as mentoring, feedback, observations, and professional development (Winstead Fry, 2010; Aitken et al., 2008).

Background

Early childhood education programs within post-secondary institutions rely on relationships between the student, the early childhood education instructor, and the sponsor educator. The early childhood education instructor is someone who teaches in a post-secondary institution, and the sponsor educator is the educator who is supporting the student in their practicum by modeling skills, observing the student, and providing feedback. The sponsor educator and the early childhood education instructor spend many hours with the early childhood education student, discussing matters of pedagogy and issues of practice, such as how to guide children's behavior (Rodd, 2013). With the assistance of the sponsor educator and the instructor, the student takes on increasing levels of responsibility. The student is given feedback on a consistent basis and is supported in making any necessary changes to their practice.

As mentioned earlier, the length of education for early childhood educators varies internationally, as does the support to them as they enter the profession. In New Zealand, early childhood educators are assigned a mentor who is involved in providing professional development, observation, feedback, and assessments during a two-to-five-year period prior to educators applying for fully registered teacher status (Aitken et al., 2008). Early childhood educators viewed the program as being "vital to the profession and to the eventual completion of their teaching registration" (p. 25). In the United States, the Early Childhood Professional Mentoring Group (ECPMG) has been created to support educators as they enter the field of inclusive education (Recchia & Puig, 2019). The group relies on peer support, collective problem-solving, and ongoing reflection to help educators as they transition into practicing educators. In this study, peers have been found to be a powerful influence when it comes to providing induction support. A coaching team in the south of England is based on the statutory requirement in the Early Years Foundation Stage (Department for Education, 2017), "for all staff to have regular supervision or professional conversations" (Poulter Jewson, 2020, p. 136). The professional conversations utilize both mentoring and coaching to support educators in reflection and goal setting. The impacts of professional conversations include time for reflection and discussion, the workplace environment, the ongoing development of professionalism, and the individual's beliefs about themselves (Poulter Jewson, 2020). In contrast, in Canada there is no defined structure to support early childhood educators at the beginning of their careers, a time when they may possibly need it the most (Rodd, 2013).

The Workplace Context in which Novice Early Childhood Educators Are Involved

In order to understand the needs of novice early childhood educators, it is important to identify the issues at play within the work environment. These include the high turnover of staff, educator burnout, first year characterized as "survival," directors without increased education, and lack of government funding for early learning programs. These are depicted visually in Figure 0.1. These issues will be discussed within the broader topics of the working environment and leadership in early childhood education.

The Working Environment for Early Childhood Educators in British Columbia

Beginning early childhood educators are hired into a variety of positions such as infant-toddler child care, campus-based child care, school-age child care, Strong

Figure 0.1 Issues facing novice early childhood educators. © Laura K. Doan.

Start programs, parent cooperative nursery schools, laboratory/demonstration nursery schools, teen-parent programs, head start programs, family resource centers, and play therapy programs (Mayfield, 2001). Beginning early childhood educator roles include "nurturer; facilitator, guide and instructor; model; program and curriculum organizer; observer and evaluator; learner and researcher; and colleague and professional" (Mayfield, 2001, p. 115). As there is no formal structure for supporting novice early childhood educators, there may or may not be adequate support to mentor them through their survival year, a term Katz (1972) used to describe an early childhood educator's first year, a time when they are simply trying to make it through the day or week.

The early childhood education field is one where there is a high turnover of staff, and early childhood educators are elevated to positions of leadership when they may not be prepared (Kwon et al., 2020; McMullen et al., 2020; Bella & Bloom, 2003). In British Columbia, currently, there are close to 22,972 certified early childhood educators and 9,159 certified early childhood educator assistants (K. Reynolds, personal communication, October 13, 2022), yet we continue to have a shortage of early childhood educators both within the province of British Columbia and across Canada. According to one report, "62% of child care centre operators in Canada had to recruit staff in the last two years," and "82% had difficulty hiring staff with the necessary qualifications" (McCuaig, Akbari, & Correia, 2022). Moreover, it is estimated that up to half of all early childhood educators leave the field within the first five years, creating huge issues in retention and recruitment (Early Childhood Educators of British Columbia, 2012; CBC News, 2022). Additionally, beginning early childhood educators may find themselves working in a child care program where they are the only staff member with recognized post-secondary credentials (Doan & Gray, 2021). A constant rotation of new staff and/or very few qualified educators can lead to role ambiguity and workplace conflict, which in turn can result in burnout (Viotti et al., 2019; Ahmad, Saffardin, & Teoh, 2020; Manlove, 1993). A study by the Child Care Human Resources Sector Council confirmed a need for additional training for early childhood educators:

> Many employers indicated that they were promoted into their current role because they were good practitioners; but did not necessarily have the educational or experiential background of an "employer" or administrator. Many lacked formal HR training and learned most of the human resources/management skills required on their own. Thus, the issues that employers face are often compounded by a relative lack of knowledge and/or experience with human resources. (Kristiansen, Tholin, & Bøe, 2021; Costigliola & Peek, 2009)

Leadership in Early Childhood Education

Due to a shortage of staff, early childhood educators move quickly into positions of leadership, be they team leaders, supervisors, or directors, and many do not have adequate training or experience (Doan & Gray, 2021). Bloom (2003) found that "a director's level of formal and specialized training is a strong predictor of overall program quality, while years of directing a child care center are not as potent a predictor of quality" (p. 11). She further asserted, "it is evident that directors need much more than a learning-along-the-way kind of knowledge to be successful" (p. 11). It seems that new early childhood educators are not the only ones who experience a survival stage. Bloom (2007) maintained,

> Many, but not all, novice directors have a survival focus—a concern with "just making it". These directors may be so preoccupied with whether they are personally up to meeting the multiple demands confronting them each day that they are unable to see beyond the immediate exigencies. (p. 39)

A novice director who is experiencing what Bloom describes may have difficulty supporting early childhood educators in their first year of teaching since they may be experiencing their own form of the survival stage.

Purpose of the Book

The purpose of this book is to describe the induction experiences and needs of beginning early childhood educators and to share the theoretical framework to design a program of support for beginning early childhood educators. This book is based on current research on the induction of early childhood educators. This was original research with beginning early childhood educators in British Columbia, Canada, and was conducted by me, the author. The following research questions were addressed:

1. What are beginning early childhood educators' perceptions of their induction experiences in their first year as early childhood educators?
2. What, if any, kind(s) of induction support do beginning early childhood educators receive in their first year and how effective are these in supporting beginning early childhood educators' development of professional capacity?
3. What, if any, forms of induction or novice professional development would beginning early childhood educators like to take part in, and why?

A summary of the research is provided at the end of this introduction and includes information on the context for the research, who the participants are, and how the study was organized.

This book is based upon several assumptions: first, that early childhood education is valuable; second, that beginning early childhood educators experience some level of difficulty in their first year of teaching and that this has negative effects on children; and third, that there are induction processes that could be put in place to support beginning early childhood educators. In addition, this book is based on the assumption that beginning early childhood educators require some level of support in their first year of work. For the purposes of this book, support is defined as instruction related, where early childhood educators are aided with the necessary knowledge, skills, and strategies necessary for success in the early childhood education program, and as psychological support, where the beginning educator receives help in understanding their new role and in handling stress (Gold, 1996).

Significance of the Book

The quality of early childhood programs is directly linked to the quality of the early childhood educators working in the program (Rodd, 2013). Thus, when beginning early childhood educators are not properly inducted into the profession, the quality of early childhood education programs suffers, and the needs of children are not met. For example, early childhood educators may have difficulty connecting theory to practice (Rodd, 2013); they may experience exhaustion (Viotti et al., 2019; Ahmad, Tholin, & Bøe, 2020; Manlove, 1993), and some may leave the profession completely (McCuaig, Akbari, & Correia, 2022; Kwon et al., 2020; Early Childhood Educators of British Columbia, 2012). The information in this book, which includes theories of educator development and current research on the induction of early childhood educators, has the potential to be significant for beginning early childhood educators, sponsor educators, administrators, early childhood education faculty, researchers, and policymakers. Potential benefits, implications for practice, implications for policy, and implications for research are discussed here.

Potential Benefits

The information shared in this book could lead to a better understanding of what is necessary to successfully induct early childhood educators into the profession and this could lead to early childhood educators staying in the field for longer periods of time, a greater connection between theory and practice, and ultimately a higher quality early childhood education program for children. A study in New Zealand (Aitken et al., 2008) found that part of the role of mentors was to teach novice early childhood educators how to teach, how to be part of the teaching profession, and what to do if one feels discouraged because the anticipated career goals are not met. In short, early childhood educators were mentored into the profession and were helped to avoid burnout.

Implications for Policy

Early Childhood Educators of British Columbia (ECEBC), the provincial organization representing early childhood educators, has stated in their *Community Plan for a Public System of Integrated Early Care and Learning* (2019) document that a Bachelor of Early Childhood Education should become the standard for all early childhood educators, and this has resulted in considerable pressure on institutions in British Columbia to offer full degrees in early childhood education. As the Early Childhood Educators of British Columbia work toward changing the policies regarding educational requirements, results from this research could help to inform policies designing effective curriculum for early childhood educators. Additionally, the information shared in this book could lead to a greater understanding of what specifically leadership in early childhood education is, and this could lead to a recognition of the importance of supporting first-year early childhood educators. Along with moving toward a Bachelor of Early Childhood Education as the standard, it is possible that the Early Childhood Educators of British Columbia would create a policy similar to New Zealand (Aitken et al., 2008), where first-year early childhood educators are assigned a mentor for their first year of teaching.

Implications for Practice

The information shared in this book could help to determine what kind of education is needed for early childhood educators in leadership positions, such as supervisor, team leader, or director, and this could lead to changes in current education available in colleges and universities in British Columbia, as well as in other jurisdictions, worldwide, such as new courses being offered. Aitken et al. (2008) recommended that "some form of manual or guidelines for inclusion is provided to Provisionally Registered Teachers" (p. x) and that "future resourcing and education of mentor teachers would help" (p. 39). Results from this study may be used for curriculum development regarding ways to support beginning early childhood educators. Additionally, the results may provide a strong rationale for a mentor or peer support program, such as the one discussed in a paper on the benefits of peer mentoring for educators (Kupila & Karila, 2019). Furthermore, Katz (1972) characterized the first year of an early childhood educator as "survival," but does this have to be? If beginning early childhood educators experience an induction process that may include mentoring or peer coaching, could their first year be one where they thrive? Additionally, could retention of new early childhood educators be improved?

Implications for Research

Currently, there is a disparity between early childhood educators and those who conduct research, and Rodd (2006) asserted that this is due to a lack of ownership on the part of early childhood educators. Within the early childhood education field, there are many who make decisions from a "subjective viewpoint, which is usually derived from personal values and experience" (p. 202), a reliance on intuition rather than theory. Rodd argued for a different approach, one where early childhood educators "engage in research that links practice to professional knowledge" and find that research can in fact be used as a "major source of information" in decision-making (p. 205).

According to Thornton et al. (2009), "the lack of research focusing on leadership in ECE provides a contrast to the abundance of literature relating to leadership in the school sector" (p. 5). In addition, the OECD (Douglass, 2019) has identified a lack of research on leadership within early childhood education as well as a lack of support for leadership development in early childhood education. This study could inform future research into the induction of beginning early childhood educators and may in fact contribute to the building of theory about ways to support first-year early childhood educators. A study done on teacher induction in New Zealand (Aitken et al., 2008) recommended that further research be done on mentoring models in early childhood education.

As mentioned previously, many early childhood educators do not value research, seeing it as something that is not relevant to their practice (Rodd, 2013). Rodd highlighted the importance of educators having a sense of ownership in the research, which can happen when educators are involved in the research and are viewed as collaborators: "early childhood educators should increasingly be

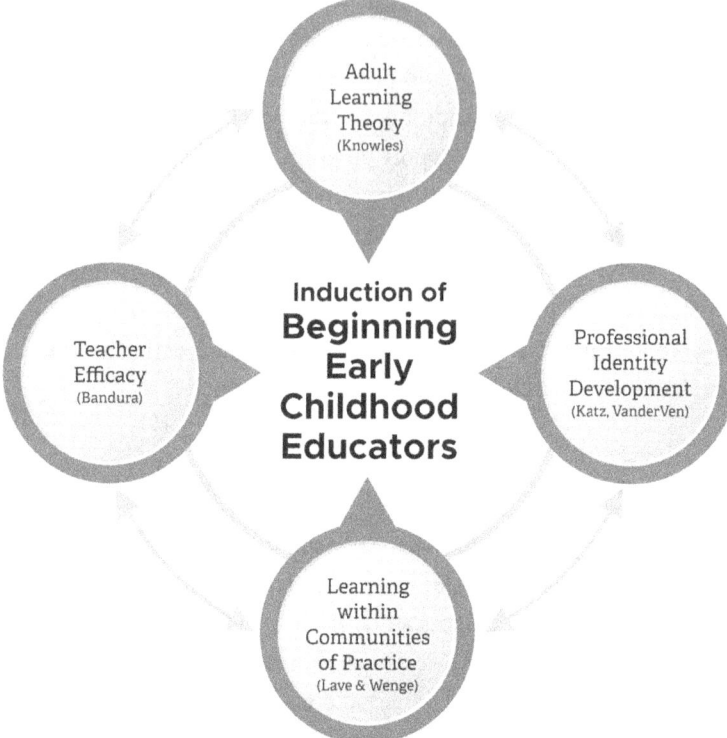

Figure 0.2 Theoretical framework. © Laura K. Doan.

active in research because of the added value brought about by systematic inquiry into practice" (p. 212). Furthermore, Rodd stated, "Collaborative research plays an important role in enhancing critical reflection and co-construction of professional understanding because it offers educators opportunities to engage in conversations about pedagogy and change in knowledgeable and meaningful ways" (p. 212). Participatory research of the kind shared in this book could help early childhood educators to see the value of research in informing practice, and this could lead to early childhood educators being open to participating in future research endeavors.

Theoretical Framework

This book explores how beginning early childhood educators are transitioning into working within their professional workplace. The aim of this research was to develop understanding of beginning early childhood educators' experiences and their needs. Specifically, are they able to make this transition successfully and with ease, not as static acceptors of current professional culture, but as positive influencers of change? The theoretical framework for this study, as depicted visually in Figure 0.2, draws upon current theories of learning in professional workplaces as well as general theories of learning. As this study involved adults, Knowles' adult learning theory provided a theoretical context to how adults learn and more specifically what motivates them and how they can be taught in a way that meets their needs. The theories of professional identity development put forth by Katz (1972) and Vander Ven (1988) are pivotal to this work as the participants of this study are in the beginning stages of their career, trying to develop their professional identity. Lave and Wenger's (1991) community of practice theory fits well here given the early childhood education workplace and educational context where educators do not receive consistent professional development and/or ongoing training. This theory provides a theoretical base from which workplace support can be considered. Teacher efficacy, which comes from Bandura's (1997) work, helped to inform the study in a variety of ways, including why some educators remain in the profession and why others choose to leave.

In Figure 0.2, the induction of novice early childhood educators, which is central to the research presented, is centered in the middle. Circling this large circle are four smaller circles, each representing a different theory: adult learning theory, professional identity development, communities of practice, and teacher efficacy. The double-sided arrows are placed in between each of the circles to represent that these theories do not stand alone. Rather, in the context of this research, each one has the capacity to influence and inform the other. For example, a teacher's level of efficacy, how they perceive their abilities as a teacher, impacts their ability to develop their professional identity. If an early childhood educator is unable to move past Katz's survival stage, they may not develop the necessary level of teacher efficacy and may leave the profession. Moreover, adult learning theory informs and influences the learning that can take place within communities of practice. Is an adult ready to learn? Is there a motivation to learn based on intrinsic reasons? And can this learning occur within a community of practice? That is, if the novice early childhood educator is both ready and motivated to learn, he or she is poised to receive the learning she needs on the jobsite. However, is the jobsite one that is viewed as a community of practice? Is there another community of practice that the novice early childhood educator is involved in? Knowles (2012) suggested the best learning situations are those where adults have some control, and this concept fits well with a community of practice in that it evolves from the ground up and is not a forced practice from administrators. What happens to the novice early childhood educator if their learning needs are not met? How does this impact his or her teacher efficacy? By these examples, one can see the important links between the four theories. More detail on each of the theories will be provided in Chapter 1.

Structure of the Book

The book is organized into two parts, with eight chapters. Part I looks at the educators' experiences in the first five years of work, focusing on research with early childhood educators. Part II, "Moving Forward," looks at a best practice for early childhood educators, as well as theories and new directions in early childhood education. What follows next is a summary of the research, as well as how the research shapes the content of the book.

Summary of the Original Research Undertaken (Doan, 2014)

Research Questions

1. What are beginning early childhood educators' perceptions of their induction experiences in their first year as early childhood educators?
2. What, if any, kind(s) of induction support do beginning early childhood educators receive in their first year and how effective are these in supporting beginning early childhood educators' development of professional capacity?
3. What, if any, forms of induction or novice professional development would beginning early childhood educators like to take part in, and why?

Participants

This study drew from the population of certified early childhood educators from the province of British Columbia who had been working in the early childhood education field for five years or less. Specific information on the participants is shared in Table 0.2.

Table 0.2 Demographic Characteristics of Participants ($N = 114$)

		N	%
Gender			
	Female	110	96.5
	Male	4	3.5
Age			
	18–24	28	24.6
	25–34	51	44.7
	35–44	23	20.2
	45–54	9	7.9
	55–64	3	2.6
Experience in the Field			
	1 year or less	31	27
	2 years	20	17.5
	3 years	24	21
	4 years	20	17.5
	5 years	19	17
Highest Level of Education			
	Certificate	45	39.5
	Diploma	19	16.7
	Post-Diploma Certificate	33	28.9
	Bachelor's Degree	14	12.3
	Master's Degree	3	2.6
Number of ECE Staff			
	1	6	5
	2	21	18
	3	18	16
	4 or more	70	61
Location of the Program			
	The Islands	16	14.03
	Vancouver Coast and Mountains	48	42.1
	Thompson Okanagan	31	27.2
	BC Rockies	3	2.63
	Northern British Columbia	7	6.14
	Cariboo Chilcotin	9	7.9
Type of Area			
	Rural	19	16.7
	Urban	55	48.2
	Metropolitan	40	35.1

Methods

I used both quantitative and qualitative methods in a quest to fully understand the induction experiences and needs of novice early childhood educators. The research involved both an online questionnaire through Survey Monkey and face-to-face or telephone interviews with me, the researcher, the purpose being to involve as many beginning educators as possible while eliciting in-depth interviews through a semi-structured format.

Sampling: Purposeful sampling was used to identify beginning early childhood educators within this population who met specific criteria. Purposeful sampling is where the researcher chooses participants who have experience with the phenomenon being explored (Creswell & Plano Clark, 2007). The criteria for selection included early childhood educators who have been working in the early childhood education field for five years or less. In other words, this study was only open to participants who held valid early childhood education post-secondary training.

Research ethics: Best practice in ethical research was used following guidelines from the Canadian Government Tri-Agencies Council on Research. Prior to beginning research, ethical approval was obtained from Thompson Rivers University Research Ethics Board.

Data collection: As the purpose of this study was to explore the induction experiences and needs of beginning early childhood educators, a qualitative approach was utilized whereby educators' experiences were elicited. Denzin and Lincoln (2005) described the interview as a powerful way to understand the experiences of others. Interviews can take place face-to-face or via the telephone, with individuals or with groups. The interviews were conducted with eleven participants who contacted me, the researcher. The study involved qualitative semi-structured interviews in which participants were asked to answer eleven predetermined interview questions. For example:

1. Tell me about your first experiences as an early childhood educator.
2. Can you tell me about the kinds of support you have received as a beginning early childhood educator?
3. Have you received the support you felt you needed? Why (or why not)?
4. Induction is a time when an early childhood educator is introduced to the field of early childhood education. Activities may include mentoring, professional development, observations, and feedback on practice (Piggot-Irvine et al., 2009). Given this definition of induction, would you say you were involved in induction activities as a new early childhood educator? If so, what induction activities did you take part in?

The questionnaire used in this study was derived from Magill (2002) and Ozgun (2005) who researched beginning teachers in Alberta, Canada, and beginning early childhood educators in Turkey. The online questionnaire began with an explanation to subjects of the purpose of the study. Following this an informed consent statement was shared in which potential participants were asked to make a decision about their participation. If participants clicked "I agree" to the informed consent statement, they were agreeing to participate in the study, allowing the researcher (me) to use their data. Early childhood educators who clicked "I do not agree" were taken to a final page where they were thanked for their time and consideration of the study. Participants who agreed to take part in the study were taken to the next screen where the first questions appeared. Demographic information was collected first. This included age, qualification level, years in the field, area of British Columbia in which they are located, identification of rural, urban, or inner city designation, number of early childhood educators in their workplace, and type of early childhood education program.

There were both closed and open-ended questions. The closed questions were based on the following scales: adjustment to the early childhood education program; adjustment to the early childhood education classroom; adjustment to the field of early childhood education; adjustment to the new role; adjustment to supervisory practices; and adjustment to administrative practices. These questions involved a five-point Likert scale where beginning early childhood educators were asked to rate the level of support they needed and the level of support received. Following this were questions related to job satisfaction. At the end of each scale, including the section on job satisfaction, participants had an opportunity to share additional information related to the scale. There were three open-ended questions at the end of the questionnaire:

- Other experiences that have contributed to your adjustment to the role of an early childhood educator;
- From the questionnaire, what are the three most important things you think contribute to early childhood educators' adjustment to their role?; and
- Is there anything else you would like to share about your experiences as a beginning early childhood educator?

Pseudonyms have been used to present from the data.

Data analysis: As this was a mixed methods study, qualitative and quantitative data were analyzed in different ways. All interviews were transcribed verbatim and participants received copies of their transcripts in order to review for accuracy. For the semi-structured interviews, the researcher I used a process of data condensation through the use of codes (Miles, Huberman, & Saldana, 2014). Prior to the start of data collection, provisional codes were assigned using the research questions, conceptual framework, and codes and themes used in similar research studies on beginning early childhood educators (Miles, Huberman, & Saldana, 2014). These codes included reality shock, preservice teaching experiences, philosophical differences, lack of time, workload, and support, and were used for the first-level coding of all interview data. This phase of coding was meant as a starting point only and the researcher remained open to further codes that emerged from the data, something that is consistent with this form of coding (Miles, Huberman, & Saldana, 2014). Second-level coding began with additional codes emerging.

The online questionnaire included mostly quantitative data with several open-ended response questions as part of the mixed methods approach. The open-ended questions were analyzed in the same way as the interview data, with the assigning of provisional codes and then secondary coding. As with the qualitative interview data, the researcher added to the provisional codes as additional codes emerged from the data. Using SPSS software, I analyzed the Likert scale questions under each cluster to determine in what area beginning early childhood educators require and receive the most support. Descriptive statistics were provided for all questions and this included measures of central tendency: the mean, mode, and median responses. Descriptive statistics can be categorized numerically, such as "measures of central tendency and variability" and graphically, through the use of "histograms, bar charts, and scatter plots" (Given, 2008, p. 209).

Results

In Part I of the book, I present the key findings from 11 interviews and 114 questionnaires.

Beginning with the online questionnaire, I provide descriptive statistics on the following six scales:

- Adjustment to early childhood education program (Chapter 2);
- Adjustment to early childhood classroom (Chapter 3);
- Adjustment to the field of early childhood education (Chapter 3);
- Adjustment to new role (Chapter 2);
- Adjustment to supervisory practices (Chapter 4); and
- Adjustment to administrative practices (Chapter 4).

The highest level of need was found to be under the adjustment to the new role, where between 25 percent and 53 percent of beginning early childhood educators reported receiving less than what they needed. Specific questions related to induction activities such as feedback, observations, professional development, and mentoring were tallied and according to reports from beginning early childhood educators in this study, 49 percent to 52 percent received no or little induction support, the average being 49 percent. While many beginning early childhood educators receive the support they need, 30 percent to 50 percent do not. Descriptive statistics are provided for the job satisfaction measure and show that despite these potential challenges, job satisfaction is quite high, with 89 percent of beginning early childhood educators reporting good or very good satisfaction with their job.

Results from the interviews are organized and presented around each of the three research questions: (1) What are beginning early childhood educators' perceptions of their induction experiences in their first year as early childhood educators? (2) What, if any, kind(s) of induction support do beginning early childhood educators receive in their first year and how effective are these in supporting beginning early childhood educators' development of professional capacity? (3) What, if any, forms of induction or novice professional development would beginning early childhood educators like to take part in, and why?

Research question one (What are beginning early childhood educators' perceptions of their induction experiences in their first year as early childhood educators?) is answered through the themes of "preparedness" and "philosophy," with participants sharing their experiences as early childhood educators. This is in Chapter 2.

For research question two (What, if any, kind(s) of induction support do beginning early childhood educators receive in their first year and how effective are these in supporting beginning early childhood educators' development of professional capacity?), the theme of "lack of support" was determined. However, this does not mean that support was not received. Participants talked about support around the themes of "support from the jobsite" and "support from the community." The theme of "inconsistent induction support" arose from the data, but some participants did experience aspects of induction and these were grouped around "induction activities." Furthermore, participants identified the helpfulness of "workplace support," "preservice experiences," "community experiences," and "support from coworkers." When describing the likelihood of the participants continuing in the early childhood education field, the theme of "unpredictable future" was identified. This is included in Chapter 4.

The third and final research question (What, if any, forms of induction or novice professional development would beginning early childhood educators like to take part in, and why?) is answered through the main theme of "early childhood educators want support for new early childhood educators." The following themes emerged as specific ways of supporting new early childhood educators: "mentoring," "introductions," "professional development," "supportive work environment," and "support from the early childhood education community." Italics have been used to indicate the use of direct quotations from the participants of the study. This is included in Chapter 5.

Organization of the Book

Chapter 1: Theories and Practices Related to the Development of Educators

This chapter provides a review of the literature that is based on the theoretical framework of the study, the theoretical basis for the research with new early childhood educators. As this research involved educators who were involved in teaching and learning, the following theories are part of the theoretical framework and will be covered in this chapter: professional identity development (Katz, 1972; Vander Ven, 1988), teacher efficacy (Bandura, 1997), adult learning theory (Knowles, Holton, & Swanson, 2012), and communities of practice (Lave & Wenger, 1991). In addition, literature on coaching and mentoring is provided, as it relates to induction-related activities for novice early childhood educators.

Part I: Educators' Experiences in the First Five Years of Work

Chapter 2: The New Role

This chapter begins with information on the context for the role of the early childhood educator. From there, results are shared on the role of the early childhood educator. First, information is shared from a survey. Second, responses are shared from open-ended ended questions from the survey, and third, information is shared related to the first research question (What are beginning early childhood educators' perceptions of their induction experiences in their first year as early childhood educators?), from the qualitative interview. Starting with percentages and ending with qualitative quotes enables a fulsome picture of what support is received and what can be helpful for new early childhood educators as they navigate the new role.

Chapter 3: Adjusting to the Field of Early Childhood Education

This chapter begins with information on the context for the field of early childhood education. From there, results are shared on the adjustment to the early childhood education classroom, the adjustment to the field of early childhood education, and job satisfaction. I share information from the survey completed by new early childhood educators. Following this, responses are shared from the open-ended questions from the survey. Finally, information is shared related to the first research question: What are beginning early childhood educators' perceptions of their induction experiences in their first year as early childhood educators?, from the qualitative interview. Starting with percentages and ending with qualitative quotations helps to provide a clear picture of what support is received and what can be helpful for new early childhood educators as they navigate the field of early childhood education. In addition, hearing from educators on their perspectives related to job satisfaction provides insight as they are at their most ideal or optimistic stage.

Chapter 4: Supervisory Practices

This chapter begins with information on the context for supervisory practices. From there, results are shared from the perspectives of beginning early childhood educators. First, information is shared from a survey. Second, responses are shared from open-ended ended questions from the survey, and third, information is shared related to the second research question (What, if any, kind(s) of induction support do beginning early childhood educators receive in their first year and how effective are these in supporting beginning early childhood educators' development of professional capacity?), from the qualitative interview. Starting with percentages and ending with qualitative quotes enables a fulsome picture of what support is received and what can be helpful for new early childhood educators as they navigate the new role.

Chapter 5: Induction Support

This chapter begins with information on the context for induction support. From there, results are shared from the perspectives of beginning early childhood educators. First, information is shared from a survey. Second, responses are shared from open-ended ended questions from the survey, and thirdly, information is shared related to the third research question (What, if any, forms of induction or novice professional development would beginning early childhood educators like to take part in, and why?), from the qualitative interview. Starting with percentages and ending with qualitative quotes provides a complete understanding of what kinds of induction support are received, and this can provide insight into beginning early childhood educators want in their first year (or more) of work.

Chapter 6: Key Themes

In this chapter, the key themes are presented in relationship to findings from the literature as well as the theories from the theoretical framework. This helps to provide the scholarly context within which the themes can be viewed. Finally, within each theme a critique will be offered, highlighting where the findings differ from the current literature.

Part II: Moving Forward

Part I focused on the experiences of early childhood educators in the first five years of work. In the next section of the book, Part II, we look at implications and recommendations through the lens of best practice for early childhood educators. Additionally, theories and new directions for early childhood education will be discussed, with an aim to show what is possible when we work alongside early childhood educators, listening to them and positioning them as the experts.

Chapter 7: Toward a Best Practice for Early Childhood Educators

This chapter begins with a discussion of the major findings and conclusions drawn from this research study. This includes the introduction of new knowledge through models of how beginning early childhood educators are perceived as well as additions to the theory of educator development. This is followed by recommendations, which include the introduction of the Doan Model for Best Practice for the Induction of Beginning Early Childhood Educators and subsequent implications for further research, ECEBC (the Early Childhood Educators of British Columbia), government policy, and post-secondary institutions.

Chapter 8: Theories and New Directions in Early Childhood Education

This chapter builds on what has been shared previously and provides insight into future research, including a peer mentoring program for early childhood educators. Educator well-being is critical, not only for the educators themselves but also for children, families, the early learning workplace, and society in general, as it is related to an educators' ability to remain in the early learning field, with a commitment to the profession (Grant, Jeon, & Buettner, 2019). With this in mind, in this chapter, I provide information on new directions in both research and programs of support for early childhood educators, with the intention of bringing into fruition the aspirations of educators.

1

Theories and Practices Related to the Development of Educators

Professional Identity Development

When attempting to understand the needs of novice early childhood educators, it can be helpful to draw upon theories of educator development. Katz (1972) proposed a theoretical model for the stages of early childhood educators. The first stage, survival, as its name suggests, is where the educator simply tries to get through the day or week, and this can last up to one year. Katz wrote, "During this period the teacher needs support, understanding, encouragement, reassurance, comfort and guidance. She needs instruction in specific skills and insight into the complex causes of behaviour—all of which must be provided on the classroom site" (p. 4). What is key here is the on-site support the beginning early childhood educator requires, making it important that the mentor is physically nearby to assist the educator in daily situations, such as how to guide children's behavior, form connections with family members, and plan programming based on children's needs and interests. Veenman (1984) and others (Correa, Martínez-Arbelaiz, & Aberasturi-Apraiz, 2015; Mahmood, 2013) have described the transition into one's first teaching position as being a "reality shock," where teachers can experience vast differences between what they idealized in their teacher training versus the reality of the classroom. In addition to being introduced to the teaching profession, the novice teacher may also be dealing with the realities of living in the adult world, which may include leaving home and transitioning into a new community (Veenman, 1984). Moreover, cognitive development plays a role in the development of a professional identity as teachers who are at a higher developmental level are better able to adapt to the demands placed upon them. A study in the UK found that most of the childcare students and staff were young: "around 70 percent of the students were aged between 16 and 19; and the average age for nursery staff was 24 years old and for nursery heads was 40 years" (Cameron et al., 2001, p. 18).

Katz (1972) went on to describe stage two: consolidation, a phase when educators are "consolidating overall gains made during the stage and to differentiate specific tasks and skills to be mastered next" (p. 5). This period is one where educators feel more confident and are able to focus less on themselves and more on the individual needs of the children. Katz described the third and fourth stages, renewal and maturity, as times when educators are seeking further professional development and asking some of the deeper questions about topics such as philosophy and how change occurs. When comparing Katz's model of educator development to Veenman (1984) one question is, do all early childhood educators proceed to stage two, three, or four? Approximately half of all beginning early childhood educators in British Columbia will leave the profession in the first five years (Early Childhood Educators of British Columbia, 2012). A recent report on the workforce in British Columbia found that more new early childhood educators have left the early childhood education field (Social Research and Demonstration Corporation, 2021). Of those that remain, do they pass through the stages, getting to a place of maturity as described by Katz? According to Veenman, the influence of teacher training is weakened by the daily teaching experiences, and in some cases, teachers who become more conservative in their first year of teaching do not revert back to the liberalization of their training. In 2007, the Early Childhood Educators of British Columbia wrote a report entitled, *Developing a Strategy for Professional Leadership* where they reported, "a mentoring framework is needed to help people take steps to be mentors" (Gay 2007, p. 18). Additionally, it was suggested that Katz's (1972) developmental stages of early childhood educators be explored. A study in New Zealand found evidence of the positive impact of mentoring within a supportive workplace community (Whatman, 2016). Furthermore, the OECD has suggested that teacher development be viewed as a continuum, with teachers receiving support at the beginning of their career in addition to ongoing professional development (OECD, 2005). It is possible that induction activities such as feedback, observations on practice, professional development, and peer coaching or mentoring could be useful strategies in helping beginning early childhood educators to successfully enter the profession.

Vander Ven (1988) has identified five stages of professionalism that are tied to the experience, roles, and level of education: novice, initial, informed, complex, and influential. Early childhood educators in the first two stages require a great deal of direction and supervision in their work, and unfortunately, they may not receive the support required due to the high turnover of staff (Nicholson & Reifel, 2011). Both Katz (1972) and Vander Ven have developed models based largely on Piaget, whereas some such as Fleet and Patterson (2001) reject the notion of development through stages, asserting a Vygotskian approach, where practitioners learn from each other.

Teacher Efficacy

Self-efficacy is one part of Bandura's social cognitive theory and is related to an individual's beliefs about their own power to create change (Bandura, 1997). It is less about one's skills and more to do with what one thinks one is able to accomplish. Bandura posited the idea that "beliefs of personal efficacy constitute the key factor of human agency" (p. 3). In other words, people who believe they have the power to create change will attempt to do so. Bandura believed people are not simply products of their environments. Rather, they are seen as agents who have the power to act, based on what they believe they can do. Teacher efficacy is a term that refers to a teachers' belief in their own ability to carry out teaching tasks with success (Tschannen-Moran, Woolfolk Hoy, & Hoy, 1998). Early childhood educators who have a strong sense of teacher efficacy are open to new ideas, are better able to plan, demonstrate greater enthusiasm for teaching, have a strong commitment to teaching, and are more likely to stay in the profession (Ozgun, 2005). Early childhood educators need to feel important, to believe they are making a difference. Teachers with high efficacy believe they can help all students, including the ones who struggle academically, and they will make the necessary efforts, while teachers with low efficacy may take a more custodial role and attribute the lack of student achievement to a variety of outside influences, including a lack of family involvement (Bandura, 1997). An early childhood educator with low teacher efficacy then may think they are powerless to make a change, resulting in less effort in curriculum planning, for example. Whitebrook and Sakai (2003) found that when early childhood educators feel undervalued, the quality of their work suffers, resulting in poor quality programming for children. Given that early childhood educators in British Columbia do not receive the same level of respect as school teachers, high levels of teacher efficacy may be even more important. Bandura (1993) posited that individuals with strong beliefs in their efficacy persevere through difficult circumstances to find ways of exercising control, while those with low self-efficacy beliefs embrace negative thinking and give up with little effort. Instead of working actively to solve problems, teachers with low efficacy become less engaged from teaching activities, focusing inward on their feelings of distress.

If this becomes a pattern, teachers may experience "emotional exhaustion, depersonalization, and a growing sense of futility," which can lead to burnout (Bandura, 1997, p. 242). In Switzerland, researchers have studied the burnout symptoms of early childhood educators and have found that one contributing factor is the sheer number of simultaneous tasks that educators must complete at the same time (Blochlinger & Bauer, 2018) and this concurs with research in Estonia that found teachers who worked in schools with lower numbers of children had higher efficacy (Meristo & Eisenschmidt, 2014). Looking at educator efficacy is important because Knoblock and Whittingdon (2002) found that beginning teachers who demonstrated a higher sense of efficacy were more likely to stay in the profession. Could it be that low teacher efficacy is a critical factor in the high numbers of educators leaving the field?

How Teacher Efficacy Develops

Bandura (1997) claimed that mastery of an activity is one of the most powerful influences on efficacy as it provides "authentic evidence" about whether the person has the skills necessary to be successful or not (p. 80). This concurs with a study by Knoblock and Whittingdon (2002) who found that beginning teachers who received "positive feedback, support, guidance, and encouragement" were more confident and had higher efficacy (p. 332). Moreover, Skaalvik and Skaalvik (2009) found that a positive relationship between job satisfaction and teacher efficacy existed. In order for early childhood educators to have high teacher efficacy, it is important that they be given preservice and workplace experiences whereby they receive feedback, support, and guidance on their mastery of the skills necessary to be an early childhood educator. It seems critical then for early childhood educators to have sponsor educators, post-secondary instructors, supervisors, and/or coworkers who are able to model problem-solving by demonstrating how to plan programs for children during the everyday challenges that arise in a busy childcare program. This fits well with research on novice teachers that found differences in self-efficacy and the reality of the teaching experience, making the induction year a critical time for mentoring, observations, and modeling (Gamborg et al., 2018). Additionally, the collective efficacy of the teaching team may play a role in one's personal level of teacher efficacy. Collective efficacy refers to people's "shared belief in their collective power to produce desired results," and this is an important factor in collective agency (Bandura, 2001, p. 14). As early childhood educators typically work in teams, with several educators in the same program with children, does collective efficacy influence a beginning early childhood educator's teacher efficacy? Furthermore, education, experience, and support can help teachers to feel more effective and be better teachers. Some of the factors that influenced the efficacy of beginning teachers were: "a) support and feedback; b) knowledge and education; c) teaching and student teacher experience; d) positive interactions with students; e) intrinsic motivation; f) isolation, overwhelmed and helplessness; and g) workload and unrealistic expectations" (Knobloch & Whittington, 2002, p. 331). From this study, there are many possible ramifications for early childhood educators, including opportunities for professional development and participation in induction-related activities such as mentoring and professional development.

Adult Learning Theory (Theory of Andragogy)

In contrast to Vygotsky's social learning theory that is based on children, Knowles, Holton, and Swanson (2012) believed there were inherent differences in the ways that children and adults learn, and they argued there were specific principles that must be considered when involved with adult learning. The term "andragogik" was first used in 1833 by Alexander Kapp, a German school teacher (Knowles, Holton, & Swanson, 2012). It was used to describe "the educational theory of the Greek philosopher, Plato" (p. 57). The word was forgotten for many years, and it was not until 1967 that Dusan Savicevic, a Yugoslavian educator, introduced the term "andragogy" to the American culture. It was about "the art and science of helping adults learn" and was the exact opposite of the pedagogical model (p. 59). The pedagogy is the "art and science of teaching children" (p. 60) and is based on a set of beliefs about teaching and learning. In the pedagogical model, the teacher bears all responsibility for learning and the role of the student is limited to passively going along with the teacher's instructions. Both theories of pedagogy and andragogy hold assumptions on the following: the need to know, the learner's self-concept, the role of experience, readiness to learn, orientation to learning, and motivation, but they are viewed very differently (Knowles, Holton, & Swanson, 2012). In the pedagogical model, it is assumed that learners only need to know what content they must grasp in order to pass. It is not necessary for them to know how the content can be applied to their lives. In direct contrast is the assumption from andragogy that learners need to know why they need to learn something, and this knowledge must be shared prior to the learning process. When looked at through the lens of the pedagogical model, the learner's self-concept is dependent, with an understanding that with age, the learner will be more independent (Knowles, Holton, & Swanson, 2012). As andragogy involves adult learners, it is assumed that adults are responsible for their lives and this has implications for adult education, and, in particular, in the way adult learners are engaged in directing their own learning. The experiences of the learner are not valued in a pedagogical model. Rather, the teacher's experience and abilities are viewed as important. In the theory of andragogy emphasis is placed on the experiences of the learner (Knowles, Holton, & Swanson, 2012). Understandably, adults are going to have exceedingly more experience than children simply because of their age, and according to Knowles et al. this should impact the curriculum. Instead of the teacher being viewed as an expert, knowing exactly how much scaffolding to provide, Knowles et al. suggested the adult student's experience was as equally important as the teacher's. Moreover, the learning itself was viewed as reciprocal, occurring between both the teacher and the adult students, with the students providing assistance with the curriculum. In this theory, the experiences of adults are not simply what happens to them, it is who they are (Knowles, Holton, & Swanson, 2012). For this reason, the experiences of adult learners must be taken into account in any learning situation. Following the previously mentioned passive nature inherent in the pedagogical model, readiness to learn is something that is determined by the teacher, not the students themselves. Quite the opposite is true in the andragogy model where the learners themselves are ready to learn when they see the connection to real-life situations. Additionally, learners are ready to learn when the learning tasks are associated with the next developmental level. It is important, therefore, to ensure learning situations are planned and timed according to the learner's readiness. In the pedagogical model, the learner's orientation to learning is based on acquiring subject matter content. However, in andragogy, adults are motivated to learn when they see the connections to their own lives. Last, from a pedagogical perspective, motivation is seen as external, such as grades and parental approval. While adults do respond to some external motivators, in the andragogy model, it is assumed that internal pressures are the most important motivators (Knowles, Holton, & Swanson, 2012). These may include self-esteem and increased job satisfaction. By going through the previous assumptions about learners, one can see some major differences between pedagogy and andragogy, and this was something Knowles, Holton, and Swanson (2012) suggested was necessary to fully understand the concept of andragogy.

Motivation of Adult Learners to Learn

An important assumption within the andragogy model is that of the motivation of adult learners to learn. Motivation has been described as a "natural human capacity to direct energy in the pursuit of a goal" (Wlodkowski, 2004, p. 142). Like Knowles, Holton, and Swanson (2012), Wlodkowski argued motivation comes about when adult learners view learning as "important according to their values and perspective" (p. 143). However, Long (2004) argued there is a lot of variation within adult learners, much more so than in children, and these variations can get in the way of an adult's motivation to learn. Long defined learning as a cognitive process that is influenced by the knowledge of the learner, the attitudes and beliefs held by the learner, and the emotional and/or physiological state within which the learner is situated. Adding to this complexity are personality characteristics, experiential characteristics, and role characteristics (i.e., how one behaves, how one organizes their experiences, and the roles one plays or is assigned through societal norms). In addition, Wlodkowski (2004) argued adults are culturally diverse and adults' own culture impacts their motivation to learn. For example, a person's response to a learning activity reflects his or her culture, which was defined by Wlodkowski as one's "language, beliefs, values, and behaviours" (p. 141). In any learning situation it is likely there will be many different kinds of reactions to the learning activity. For example, where one student might be challenged and feel inspired to work harder, another student facing the same obstacle may feel frustrated, wanting to give up. It is crucial then for adult educators to be sensitive to the individual needs of adult learners and to make efforts to accommodate their learning needs, choosing teaching approaches that support each adult learner.

Wlodkowski asserted the idea that responsibility on the part of the learner is of utmost importance when it comes to adult motivation. What does this mean then, for teaching adult learners? Wlodkowski established a motivational framework for culturally responsive teaching that included the following concepts: establishing inclusion, developing attitude, enhancing meaning, and engendering competence. In order for inclusion to be established, adult learners need to feel they are respected and have a connection with the group. Like Maslow, who placed importance on safety, Wlodkowski believed adults were more likely to be intrinsically motivated when they can share their opinions openly. Furthermore, when adult learners feel included in a group, they are more likely to take risks in their learning experiences. When it comes to attitude, personal relevance and choice are important, even for learners whose cultures may not value self-determination. Wlodkowski asserted the idea that learners will support the learning activities they are interested in doing. When thinking about motivating adult learners, meaning is important. Two ways to enhance meaning are through engagement and challenge. Put simply, instructors must engage learners through learning activities that are relevant to the learners themselves. Adult learners need to see that they have a purpose within the learning experience. Engendering competence is brought about through effectiveness and authenticity. Adult learners need to have feedback on their learning, which will allow them to understand their competence. The authenticity comes about through the knowledge that what one is learning is relevant to one's life. This has ramifications for assessment and as such, assignments should be seen as significant to one's life or work or career trajectory. Wlodkowski demonstrated how instructors might apply these content areas to the learning environment and some of the motivational strategies include collaborative learning, relevant learning goals, critical questioning and predicting, and self-assessment.

Learning Occurs Within Communities of Practice

Lave and Wenger (1991) put forth the theory that learning takes place within the framework of participation, not in the mind of an individual. This notion fits well with the previously mentioned ideas of learning as a construction (Wood, Smith, & Grossniklaus, 2001) and learning as a social process (Vygotsky, 1986). Lave and Wenger asserted that practitioners within communities are at work helping to bring more practitioners into the community, by way of apprenticeship. From this perspective, learning occurs through "hands-on" participation as opposed to teaching that takes place in a classroom, far removed from the workplace. Lave and Wenger's research is based on the premise that practitioners are naturally drawn to communities of practice, and their work came out of the apprenticeship experiences of tailors who became skilled master tailors through informal learning within communities of practice. Wenger and Snyder (2000) defined communities of practice as "groups of people informally bound together by shared expertise and passion for a joint enterprise" (p. 139). Wenger (2000) argued that participation in a community of practice "is essential" to learning and helps to define "what constitutes competence in a given context" (p. 229). In an early childhood education context then, through participation in a community of practice, novice early childhood educators could learn what it means to be a practicing early childhood educator. Furthermore, through participation in communities of practice, practitioners learn their identities within the community and gain belonging. Furthermore, practitioners gain an understanding of what they do in their craft. Early childhood educators are not consistently inducted into the profession in informal ways through communities of practice. For example, Nicholson and Reifel (2011) described early childhood educators' perceptions of entry training experiences as "sink or swim" (p. 5). While the early childhood educators admitted their greatest learning came from other educators, they also spoke about the lack of mentoring and the reality of being left to figure it out on their own. One participant shared: "They ended up throwing me in the classroom and just told me to go for it. That's basically what they told me" (p. 10). There are examples in other disciplines where novices learn alongside a more experienced colleague. In these cases, it is typical to have a system where the novice is identified with a particular role or title. For example, a beginning doctor takes part in a residency, where he or she begins as a first-year resident and ends as a senior resident. In contrast, in the early childhood education field, graduates enter the workplace with the same title and role as more experienced practitioners. This results in similar expectations being put on the novice as those assumed of other more senior practitioners. A researcher looking at the practica experience in Argentina found that communities of practice are a place where early childhood educators can gain knowledge of what it means to be and act professionally (Guervara, 2020).

Communities of practice are not simply for novice employees; they can benefit those with considerable experience as well (Wenger, 2000). In discussing potential benefits to organizations who use communities of practice, Wenger and Snyder (2000) reported that "communities of practice can drive strategy, generate new lines of business, solve problems, promote the spread of best practices, develop people's professional skills, and help companies recruit and retain talent" (p. 140). In this way, both novice and experienced employees can work together on a project that may involve the solving of various problems. While there are many potential benefits to communities of practice, it is interesting to note that they are not simply a practice that can be imposed upon employees in a top-down approach. Rather, communities of practice must organize themselves. However, managers can support communities of practice by bringing people together and ensuring the necessary infrastructure that support these communities is present. Some examples include the provision of time in the workday for people to meet and physical space for meetings. Unlike a workplace team where people are assigned, members of communities of practice choose to participate. Wenger and Snyder (2000) argued that communities of practice are powerful because of their ability to produce new knowledge, which helps to renew the community. However, while there seem to be many potential benefits to participation within a community of practice, there can be negative consequences as well. Communities of practice can become stagnant, resulting in a cessation of new idea creation and solving of problems. Initiative, strong relationships, and senses of belonging and the ability to reflect are critical for those in communities of practice.

While communities of practice have evolved from business, professional learning communities have come about through the field of education and have quite different aims. One of the main goals that professional learning communities seek to address is that of improving schools (Dufour, 2004). The three main ideas associated with professional learning communities are making sure that students learn, building a culture of collaboration, and focusing on results. Teachers who are involved in professional learning communities recognize the importance of working together to accomplish the common goal of learning for all students. While there is much to be gained from working together instead of working in isolation, it takes commitment and persistence on the part of teachers for professional learning communities to continue, and not all teachers want to be involved in this kind of effort. For many teachers, what happens inside their individual classrooms is still viewed as the individual teacher's concern, making efforts to collaborate challenging. In professional learning communities, it is important for teachers to be part of teams who then work on achieving learning goals that are related to the individual school and district goals. Because the over-arching goal is learning on the part of the students, it is essential for the team to see results. Dufour (2004) pointed out that professional learning communities risk dissolution when the school-based goals are not met in the established timeline. Dufour believed it was important for members of professional learning communities to have time to review and reflect on prescribed learning outcomes articulated in curriculum documents. In this way, teachers are not simply focusing on meeting a set of standards set by those in authority. It may be important to ensure that those involved in professional learning communities understand the purposes and want to participate. Additionally, it is important for teachers within a largely isolated profession to have training on *how* to collaborate. If teachers are able to address some of the barriers to collaboration, there can be rich opportunities for learning as teachers share the same assessment tools, which allows for a comparison and analysis of results. One major difference between professional learning communities and communities of practice is the informal nature of communities of practice. While professional learning communities may be initiated by school administrators with an expectation of participation, communities of practice evolve more naturally through the commonalities of individuals' interests. Further to this, in professional learning communities, the main purpose of the community has already been established: professional learning communities exist to ensure that all children learn. In contrast, the goals and subsequent initiatives of communities of practice unfold based on the interests of the individuals within the community.

Coaching

Peer coaching is a professional development strategy that promotes reciprocal learning, where the peer and the coach learn from one another (Zepeda, 2012). Peer coaching in an educational setting involves two or more colleagues who work together, helping each other to solve problems and improve practice in the workplace (Snider & Holley, 2020; Joyce, Weil, & Showers, 1992). This collective activity involves putting theory into practice and learning new skills and knowledge for the benefit of students and the educators themselves (Showers, 1985). There is more than one approach to peer coaching; peer coaches need to individualize their methods, utilizing the strategies that best suit their fellow peer's needs, interests, and abilities (Snider & Holley, 2020; Showers, 1984). For example, educators may be involved in expert coaching, where one person is considered to have more knowledge to share and may be in a position of authority. Alternatively, reciprocal coaching involves two parties helping each other, with no discernible difference in power or expertise (Donegan, Ostrosky, & Fowler, 2000). In both expert and reciprocal coaching, observations of the educator occur, with the opportunity for reflection, questioning, and future planning (Gersten, Morvant, & Brengelman, 1995). Peer coaching can take place in tandem with professional development and helps educators to apply what they are learning in concrete ways (Showers, 1985; Showers & Joyce, 1996). For example, teachers who were coached

> practiced new strategies more often and with greater skill than uncoached educators with identical initial training; adapted the strategies more appropriately to their own goals and contexts than did uncoached teachers who tended to practice observed or demonstrated lessons; retained and increased their skill over time—uncoached teachers did not; were more likely

to explain the new models of teaching to their students, ensuring that students understood the purpose of their strategy and the behaviours expected of them; and demonstrated a clearer understanding of the purposes and use of the new strategies. (Joyce & Showers, 2002, pp. 3–4)

Additionally, in order for peer coaching to be successful, it is wise for educators to receive training on how to be an effective peer coach, such as how to observe peers and give feedback on their work (Showers, 1985). Subsequent training sessions may focus on specific teaching skills and strategies that the pairs will work on together.

In peer coaching, there are benefits for both parties involved: those who are new to the teaching profession and those with experience (Showers, 1984). It is important, however, to point out how this professional development activity is different from traditional clinical supervision. For example, in this model the experienced teacher is the coach who is being observed, while the beginning teacher, the one being coached, is doing the observing (Showers & Joyce, 1996). The conversation then revolves around what was observed and the resultant lessons and tips the observer can take away and apply in his/her own practice. Additionally, peer coaching is much more than observations. It includes mutual planning, creation of learning materials, and time spent reflecting on best practices to ensure students learn. Another important distinction in this professional development strategy is that feedback and/or critique has been removed from the conversation. This has resulted in a more collaborative process that focuses on the skills to be learned and refined, rather than on the performance of either teacher. This has many results, including a more collaborative, team-like process where both parties work and learn together. For example, a novice practitioner has the opportunity to learn questioning techniques from an experienced practitioner, while the experienced practitioner can learn how to implement the latest technologies into the classroom from a novice practitioner well versed in the latest technologies (Huston & Weaver, 2008). Peer coaches reported that the greatest benefits of peer coaching were that they themselves learned the strategies they were trying to teach the peer, and peer coaches in one study perceived the benefits to themselves to outweigh those coached (Showers, 1984). In another study, educators reported the greatest benefit to be the sense of collegiality that developed among the staff (Showers, 1985; Sparks & Bruder, 1987) as teachers learned from each other through the observation process (Joyce, Weil, & Showers, 1992) and the feedback received was nonevaluative (Showers, 1985). When Showers and Joyce (1996) noticed feedback tended to be evaluative, it was removed from the peer coaching approach, which helped to ensure an even more collegial professional development strategy. Because peer coaching minimizes the power differential between the two peers, educators are willing to take risks by trying new things (Showers, 1985) and to critically reflect on their own practice by asking difficult questions (Huston & Weaver, 2008). Additionally, peer coaching can help to foster an environment within the school or childcare program where early childhood practitioners learn continually as they practice new strategies (Showers, 1985). In one study, teachers were able to minimize their own negative behaviors in favor of adopting behaviors that aided the students' learning (Peterson Miller, Harris & Watanabe, 1991). Finally, teachers who did not have access to professional development or training benefited from peer coaching (Tschantz & Vail, 2000). Teachers who engage in peer coaching have the opportunity to learn new skills in a nonthreatening approach with a peer.

There are many potential barriers to effective peer coaching, including finding time to meet (Hargreaves & Fullan, 1992; Kohler, McCullough, & Buchan, 1995), conflicting philosophies between coach and teacher (Donegan, Ostrosky, & Fowler, 2000), conflict due to gender differences (Robertson, 1992), and discord between the recommended change and the realities of the educational environment (Gersten, Morvant, & Brengelman, 1995). Additionally, feelings of inadequacy can surface for both peers, who may feel unprepared for the task of coaching (Showers, 1984), and for the teacher who may think they are being scrutinized (Gersten, Morvant, & Brengelman, 1995). Some researchers have argued to remove feedback from the process of peer coaching because peers viewed it as evaluative, which is not the purpose of feedback in this context (Showers & Joyce, 1996), but in another study participants enjoyed the increased feedback and found it to be helpful (Sparks & Bruder, 1987). Sparks and Bruder (1987) found that when everyone on staff, including the principal, took part in the peer coaching, worries about judgment were alleviated and this helped to foster a supportive climate.

It is important for the peer coaching to be focused on an area of teaching and learning that is relevant to the educator. In one study on peer coaching, novice educators did not find the peer coaching helpful as the focus was on helping the children with the most difficulty, when the novice educator was feeling overwhelmed with the day-to-day concerns of teaching (Gersten, Morvant, & Brengelman, 1995). Moreover, though teachers can learn from one another, how peer coaching is arranged makes a difference to the learning process. For example, if peer coaching is imposed on teachers, changes in practice will be fewer than those partnerships that are collaborative in nature (Hargreaves & Fullan, 1992).

It is important for educators to be proactive by communicating their needs to the peer coach, rather than assuming a passive stance where one waits for the peer coach to make decisions without input (Joyce & Showers, 1995).

Mentoring

Mentoring is similar to peer coaching in that colleagues are working together, but it is different in that one colleague, the mentor, has more experience than the other and has a role in supporting the mentee or novice in attaining the necessary knowledge and skills so they may develop as a professional (Long, 1997). Although similar to expert coaching, mentoring is different in that it is based on the relationship, rather than skills; is typically longer term than coaching; and is based on the needs of the mentee or protégé, instead of being task oriented. Early childhood educators report that a mentoring model where they connect with an experienced practitioner would be most effective as they transition into the role of a professional early childhood practitioner (Brindley, Fleege, & Graves, 2000; Whitebrook & Sakai, 1995). When asked what would help to increase their confidence, competence, and professionalism, novice teachers identified mentoring as their first priority (Ontario College of Teachers, 2006). Moreover, novice teachers recognized the following benefits of mentoring: "collaboration, feedback, observation, and sharing with experienced colleagues" (p. 8) and experiences like these can help early childhood practitioners to avoid feeling overwhelmed, isolated, and uncertain (Feiman-Nemser et al., 1999; Noble & Macfarlane, 2005). Novice early childhood educators involved in a mentoring program from the University of Worcester benefited from "support in the workplace, layers of mentoring support, relationship building, and interactions and communication" (Murray, 2006, p. 73). In contrast, early childhood educators in British Columbia are not currently involved in a formal mentoring program and are potentially left on their own during a critical time in their careers when mentoring might be beneficial. When induction programs are predicated on the belief that learning is a social process, the resulting consequence may be a culture of learning that impacts the entire workplace.

Like peer coaching, successful mentoring can result in a culture of learning, where knowledge gain occurs for both the mentor and the novice. Rodd (2006) pointed out that the early childhood profession has "endorsed informal and formal mentoring as a key leadership strategy because it focuses on helping practitioners to realize their professional potential" (p. 173). Rodd (2006) believed that most early childhood educators feel enthusiastic about their work and are eager to help others by sharing "their own knowledge, understanding, practice and expertise" (p. 173). Researchers have found that mentoring supports professional growth (Rodd, 2006), is a strategy for professional development (Kupila & Karila, 2018; Bellm & Whitebrook, 1996), helps to promote attitudes of lifelong learning (Weaver, 2004), and assists in rising above "some of the shortcomings of current approaches to training early childhood practitioners" (Rodd, 2006, p. 172). Additionally, there are opportunities for shared learning among staff groups as opposed to learning that is occurring between mentoring dyads exclusively (Murray, 2006), making mentoring an opportunity for professional development that could impact the whole workplace, resulting in increased learning and collegiality among staff (Kwon et al., 2020; Weasmer & Woods, 2003).

While mentoring has many potential benefits, as with peer coaching, there are several obstacles to successful mentoring. The issues of time and resources arise as potential barriers to mentoring programs, especially when considering an early childhood context where educators have little time for collaborative planning (Frede, 1995). In addition, building relationships is seen as a crucial piece in mentoring programs and from these relationships, mentees can be supported as they determine a plan of professional development (Heidkamp & Shapiro, 1999). Likewise, how the relationships begin is important (Long, 1997). For example, did the mentor and novice have a choice in choosing one another or was the relationship arranged by someone else? Moreover, is the relationship based on trust and respect? Adequate training of mentors is another issue that is important. If mentors are not involved in mentor training, there may be a lack of understanding regarding the mentor and novice roles, such as who is responsible for specific tasks and functions, and this can result in misunderstanding and a lack of goal completion (Long, 1997). Additionally, mentors may be excellent educators but could lack up-to-date information on innovations in the field, and if the novice appears to know more than the mentor, feelings of inadequacy or defensiveness may emerge on the part of the mentor. Mentors who have a forum to discuss the issues of pedagogy and practice may find their mentoring to be more informed. Issues of power can arise between mentors and novices as well as between mentors and other staff (Long, 1997; Rodd, 2006). For example, novice early childhood educators may be reluctant to voice concerns openly due to fears that the mentor has the power to terminate the novice educator's position and/ or to give a poor recommendation (Rodd, 2006). Mentors may inadvertently be encouraging the novice educator to work in the same style as themselves, instead of helping the novice to find the style of interaction that best suits their skill set, and due to the power difference, the mentee may choose to remain passive despite their concerns (Long, 1997). Additionally, the staff members not selected as mentors may resent those chosen for the role and depending on how this is handled, the mentor(s) may place themselves in a higher position than others in the work environment. While there are many potential benefits to learning within communities of practice, these must be well planned to avoid the possible barriers to success.

Conclusion

Identifying and addressing the needs of beginning early childhood educators is multifaceted, involving many different components including workplace environment, the early childhood educators' education, and professional development. Understanding the key concepts that underpin beginning early childhood educators' experiences and needs is vital as it provides the theoretical foundation. This chapter provided detailed information from the literature on the following theories: professional identity development, teacher efficacy, adult learning theory, and communities of practice. Additional information was shared on coaching and mentoring, which are both activities related to professional development. The next section of the book (Part I) will focus on educators' experiences in the first five years of work.

Part I

Educators' Experiences in the First Five Years of Work

2

The New Role

The work of an early childhood educator is complex, and adjusting to the role takes time. As noted in the previous chapter, professional identity development takes place over several stages. Given the shortage of early childhood educators, it is not uncommon for educators to find themselves thrown into a program, left to "sink or swim," while they try to figure out what their role is and if they can do it (Nicholson & Reifel, 2011). Unlike other jobs, an early childhood educator cannot count on having time to settle into a position and/or be assigned a mentor who can provide support and guidance. As one educator shared, she received five days of training/induction to work in a grocery store, but in her new role as an early childhood educator, she had all of the responsibilities of an early childhood educator, beginning on the first day (Doan, 2019).

Adjustment to the Early Childhood Education Program

New early childhood educators have a lot to take in when learning about the role, and this includes adjusting to the early childhood education program that one is working in. Every early learning program is different, and the differences include educational philosophy, guidance strategies, management style, equipment used, and families served. For example, new early childhood educators cannot assume they will be familiar with the approaches to guidance, programming, and communication with the children and families, even though they may have completed their full training. In this study, early childhood educators were given a survey that includes different scales that focused on specific areas related to the work of an early childhood educator. Educators were asked to reflect upon what they needed and what was received, in terms of support in adjusting to the early

Table 2.0 Adjustment to Early Childhood Education Program Scale—What Was Received

Question	Received Less	Received What Was Needed	Received More
Physical layout	17%	36.5%	46.5%
Meeting executive director (ED) or supervisor (Sup) expectations	31%	31%	38%
Understanding the program philosophy	22%	40%	38%
Learning program routines	23%	45%	32%
Forming a connection with an experienced ECE	25%	36%	39%
Becoming acquainted with staff	19%	38%	43%
Making friends with staff	15%	44%	41%
Achieving the programming goals of the ECE program	25%	41%	34%
Planning and organizing additional duties	29%	44%	27%

learning program. Individual responses were tallied to determine the number of participants who received less than what they needed, exactly what they needed, and more than what they needed, and this is displayed in Table 2.0. As seen in Table 2.0, 15–30 percent of early childhood educators in this survey reported they did not get the help they needed to adjust to the early learning program. The average from this was 23 percent. While 38 percent of participants reported receiving more than what they needed with respect to meeting the executive director or supervisor's expectations, 31 percent of participants reported receiving less than what they needed. It is interesting to note that 46.5 percent of participants reported receiving more than what they needed in the area of the physical layout of the room. With regard to forming a connection with an experienced early childhood educator, 25 percent received less than what was needed, 36 percent received what was needed, and 39 percent received more than was needed. Of those who responded by saying they received less than what was needed, 17 percent reported receiving no support and 19 percent reported receiving little support with regard to connecting with an experienced early childhood educator.

At the end of each scale, educators were given the opportunity to share anything else they might want to relate to the particular scale. Thirty percent (29) of the early childhood educators shared further thoughts on their perceived needs relating to the early childhood education program. New early childhood educators indicated they needed more support in adjusting to the type of work (both the demands and the low wage) and in particular the needs of the children. Many (9) spoke of the lack of support from staff. The following are some quotes from new early childhood educators who took part in the survey:

- *Becoming confident in my role, needing the reassurance that I'm doing a good job;*
- *Finding paid time to plan for innovative and quality child care. When you're at your ratio, there is rarely time to move beyond children's basic needs. I strongly believe quality child care needs periods of time with lower ratios especially in infant and toddler care. I also think that the lack of appreciation from supervisors and society is extremely disheartening. The general public need more education so they can appreciate the significance of our job;* and
- *Adjusting to being treated as a non-professional low wage worker.*

Given the current system in British Columbia where early childhood educators leave the post-secondary system in two to three semesters and the fact that there is limited time for program planning, it is not surprising to see concerns expressed related to needing support to gain confidence, finding paid time to plan for children's needs, and dealing with perceptions of educators from people in our society.

Adjustment to the New Role

Table 2.1 provides a visual demonstration of the individual responses related to what was received in adjusting to the new role. Between 25 percent and

Table 2.1 Adjustment to New Role—What Was Received

Question	Received Less	Received What Was Needed	Received More
Dealing with the ways ECEs are viewed by society	43%	34%	23%
Coping with the demands of administrators	42%	41%	17%
Coping with feelings of frustrations	53%	20%	27%
Coping with feelings of inadequacy	44%	26%	30%
Coping with feelings of failure	34%	38%	28%
Coping with feelings of rejection	27%	48%	25%
Celebrating feelings of joy/success	25%	33%	42%
Coping with apprehension related to the professional preparation I received through my training to become an ECE	30%	55%	15%

53 percent of beginning early childhood educators in this study indicated they did not receive the support they needed in adjusting to the new role.

It is interesting to note that for the question related to support in dealing with the ways early childhood educators are viewed by society, 43 percent of the beginning early childhood educators in this study reported they received less than what they needed in this area. Further analysis took place involving actual counts of those who reported receiving nothing or little in this area. Keeping in mind that the beginning educators could have indicated they received more than what they needed, yet received little, the results were: 23 percent received no support in this area and 39 percent received little support. The total combined number for receiving nothing or little was 63 percent. Again, it is important to note that some of the early childhood educators who indicated they received none or little still indicated they received what was needed. Additionally, when it came to receiving support in "coping with apprehension related to the professional preparation I received through my training to become an early childhood educator," 31 percent of beginning educators indicated they received no support and 33 percent reported receiving little. The combined amount for receiving no support or little support is 64 percent. Forty-four percent of beginning early childhood educators reported they did not receive the support needed with regard to dealing with feelings of inadequacy. Thirty-one percent of beginning educators reported receiving no support in this area and 34 percent reported receiving little, for a combined total of 66 percent. When asked about what was received in relation to what was needed in coping with feelings of frustration, 53 percent of beginning early childhood educators in this study reported they did not get the support they needed. Twenty-five percent of beginning educators reported receiving no support with this aspect of the new role and 33 percent reported receiving little, for a combined total of 58 percent.

Eleven new early childhood educators responded to the open-ended question related to other perceived needs relating to educators' adjustment to the new role. Comments were made related to having assertiveness skills, being flexible, and being mentored:

- *Flexibility;*
- *I was asked to take a position as a supervisor only a few months after starting working at the centre. I needed some mentorship in the transition, but I feel I did not receive any of it; and*
- *More mentoring with another ECE in the classroom would have been helpful.*

The participants acknowledged that additional skills were necessary for educators as they adjust because the new role is one that is diverse and challenging.

Additional Open-Ended Questions

At the end of the questionnaire, participants were invited to respond to three open-ended questions. These are as follows:

1. What are some other experiences that have contributed to your adjustment to the role of an early childhood educator?;
2. From the questionnaire, what are the three most important things you think contribute to early childhood educators' adjustment to their role?; and
3. Is there anything else you would like to share about your experiences as an early childhood educator?

Other Experiences that Contribute to the Adjustment of the Role of Early Childhood Educator

The first open-ended question was, "What are some other experiences that have contributed to your adjustment to the role of an early childhood educator?" Forty-two participants responded to the first question. Some participants shared more than one example. Through a process of coding, the following themes emerged:

- Preservice professional experiences (11);
- Good team (9);
- Negative experiences (9);
- Work experiences in the first year (6);
- Building relationships with families and children (5);
- Good working environment (4);
- Professional development (2);
- Having a mentor or role model (2);
- Family or friend support (2);
- Preservice personal experiences (2); and
- Personal qualities (2).

Preservice Professional Experiences

Regarding the preservice professional experiences, new early childhood educators shared experiences in early childhood education as a practicum student or substitute educator, and in non-early childhood education-related fields. Some of the quotations are included here:

- *Doing practicums in different daycares helps me to build my own philosophy and find the most effective and comfortable ways to deal with children and co-workers;*
- *I have worked as a child, youth, and family counselor for seven years in the area of mental health. This has greatly shaped how I work as a preschool teacher, and within a larger daycare organization;*
- *Experiences leading other parenting programs like Mother Goose, Nobody's Perfect; and*
- *Having excellent instructors at the college level and well educated supervisors and ECEs in the community.*

Based on these perspectives from new early childhood educators, preservice professional experiences make a positive difference to new early childhood educators as they are learning their new roles. Perhaps this experience acts as a base upon which to build.

Good Team

New early childhood educators shared specific experiences they had encountered with regard to a good team. Some shared what they valued in a good team. Examples include:

- *I am lucky enough to be a part of a team that works hard and is passionate about what we do. Going to work is enjoyable not only because of what we do, but the team you do it with;*
- *Unfortunately, I didn't have the most supportive administrator/supervisor, but I was very lucky to work with very supportive and talented educators from whom I learned a great deal!;*
- *Having a strong, caring and supportive team; and*
- *Encouragement from the early childhood educators that I work with.*

Most early childhood educators who participated in this study work on a team as opposed to on their own, but working with people does not mean there is a supportive team. New early childhood educators in this study shared the perspective that having a good team makes a difference in terms of job satisfaction. More information on job satisfaction will be shared in Chapter 3 ("Adjusting to the Field of Early Childhood Education").

Negative Experiences

New early childhood educators also identified negative experiences that have contributed to the adjustment to the role of an early childhood educator. These are feeling undervalued in work (3); unhealthy work environment (3); supervisors who are not trained (2); and dealing with the low wage (1).

New educators shared these thoughts:

- *Just poor management and supervision at my company. Thankfully I self-learn very well, but would have still loved regular feedback and support;*
- *The first year of being an early childhood educator for me was a difficult transition for me. In my case I was working with a co-worker who had graduated a year before me and were running a full preschool program. We received little to no support from the staff/owner, so we drew upon our own experiences from the early childhood education program [the training institution]; and*
- *Low pay hard to manage.*

As mentioned previously, the work of early childhood educators is challenging. The support one receives from fellow staff is dependent on the specific program and individuals who work there.

Work Experiences

New early childhood educators shared these thoughts on work experiences in the first year:

- *Subbing at a few different programs before accepting a full-time position gave me a chance to explore different philosophies and practices and see what fit best with me;*
- *Working with educators trained differently or with different levels of training; and*
- *Although school trains you, I think working in the field with real-life experiences makes you grow faster and learn real-life situations to help you in the field;*

These new educators found that diversity was something they could learn from. The early childhood education field is diverse, as individual centers and educators choose the philosophy they want to operate under. While different philosophies can create conflicts among individual early childhood educators, they can help new early childhood educators to realize their own philosophy.

Building Relationships

Building relationships with children and families is a big part of an educator's role and new early childhood educators had these thoughts:

- *Positive interactions with parents/guardians and their children, being able to watch the children from 3-5 grow and develop right before your eyes; and*
- *Hearing from happy parents and children how my work has had a positive impact.*

Early childhood educators work closely with children and families, and they want to make a difference. Feedback from children and families can help new early childhood educators to be aware of the impact they are having. In addition, the foregoing comments speak to the valuing of children and families.

Good Working Environment

Participants had this to share about having a good working environment:

- *Having well educated supervisors and educators in the community;*
- *Encouragement from the early childhood educators I work with; and*
- *Social evenings with staff.*

Early childhood educators in this study indicated the importance of a good working environment. Given the amount of time educators spend together, it is not surprising that participants value a good working environment.

Professional Development

New early childhood educators shared about the importance of professional development related to one's adjustment to the role of an early childhood educator:

- *Definitely team building exercises and going to workshops. Things that get us out as a group and as adults made us work together stronger; and*
- *Appreciate professional development. Wish I knew more about licensing and administrative roles.*

Early childhood educators who wish to renew their license to practice from the province of British Columbia must complete forty hours of professional development during a five-year period. It is not surprising then to see new educators making comments about the importance of additional professional development to support educators in their development.

Role Model or Mentor

New early childhood educators mentioned having a role model or mentor:

- *Great role models or co-educators with many years of experience; and*
- *Being able to be paired up to work with seasoned veterans of ECE was a HUGE help. If there can be anything I wish for future ECEs, it's that they work with a mentor in their first job.*

As there is no formal mentoring support for beginning early childhood educators in British Columbia, there is a recognition of the important role that experienced educators can have in supporting new educators in their first year of work.

Support from Family and/or Friends

Support from family and/or friends was viewed as important by some new early childhood educators:

- *My family's support; and*
- *The encouragement from friends.*

Early childhood education is not highly valued in our society, so some educators do not feel respected as professionals. Having the support of family and friends can help educators as they work hard in a job that has few tangible rewards.

Preservice Personal Experiences

New early childhood educators shared this about preservice personal experiences:

- *Having children of my own; and*
- *Becoming a Grandma.*

Educators bring a vast array of experiences to their work as an early childhood educator and those experiences make a difference to their adjustment.

Personal Qualities

New early childhood educators described personal qualities that might help in the adjustment to the role of early childhood educator:

- *Being creative and enthusiastic; and*
- *Work hard with all potential.*

The job of an early childhood educator is a demanding one. Individuals who possess personal qualities such as creativity, enthusiasm, and the ability to work hard will be at an advantage.

What Contributes to Early Childhood Educators' Adjustment to Their Role?

In the second open-ended question in the online questionnaire, early childhood educators were asked, "From the questionnaire, what are the three most important things you think contribute to early childhood educators' adjustment to their role?" Forty-four new educators responded, sharing their perspectives on what is the most important for early childhood educators as they adjust to their role. Through a process of coding, the following themes emerged:

- Support from administrators or supervisors (14);
- Teamwork (9);
- Being a mentor to a new early childhood educator (6);
- Support from Staff (6); and
- Professional development (5).

What follows is the themes, with corresponding quotations from new early childhood educators.

Support from Administrators or Supervisors

The majority of comments were regarding the importance of receiving support from administrators or supervisors. Participants shared the following thoughts:

- *A supportive, organized and present Administrator/Supervisor;*
- *Communication and trust with your supervisor or executive director;*
- *Connecting with their supervisors personally and professionally. Receiving help and training in administrative duties and doing many of those duties; and*
- *Strong leader to provide feedback and be able to talk to you about everything in the classroom.*

Administrators and supervisors have a big role to play within the early childhood education program. They have the opportunity to set the tone for the working environment, and the support that new early childhood educators receive.

Teamwork

Nine comments were made regarding the value of teamwork in an early childhood education workplace. New early childhood educators shared the following:

- *Learning about the philosophy of the program, working together to put the philosophy into practices, working together to create learning environment through ongoing communication;*
- *Having a team behind you who support your decisions and view you as a professional; and*
- *Feeling welcomed. Feeling valued. Feeling safe to try new things, make mistakes and discuss everything with supervisor and staff members.*

As mentioned previously, work within an early childhood education context takes place in a team environment, so being able to work effectively with others and knowing one had the support of the team is important.

Being a Mentor to a New Early Childhood Educator

Some new early childhood educators spoke about the importance of being a mentor to a new early childhood educator. Quotations from educators are included here:

- *Being a mentor to them [a new early childhood educator], supporting their decisions and recognizing the stress they are under;*
- *A good role model that puts trust and faith into you; and*
- *Having a person you can feel is a mentor who can listen to you in a non judgmental manner and provide guidance and support.*

Given the fact that there is no formal mentoring program offered to new early childhood educators, in the jurisdiction where this study took place, it is understandable that new early childhood educators in this study recognized the importance of being a mentor to new educators.

Support from Staff

New early childhood educators also identified the importance of receiving support from members of the staff. Comments include:

- *Getting to know colleagues and feeling comfortable conversing with them;*
- *Happy, helpful staff; and*
- *Support and positive regard from staff.*

New educators who shared comments in this section recognized the importance of receiving support from fellow staff members. As mentioned previously, the work of an early childhood educator typically involves working with others and receiving support from staff members is valuable.

Professional Development

Professional development was raised as an important factor in helping new educators to adjust to their role. New early childhood educators shared the following:

- *Access to/Information about continuing education opportunities (directly to the educators as sometimes information is not passed on);*
- *Continuous support for professional development; and*
- *Educational opportunities to learn about the program and its operations.*

New early childhood educators who shared examples in this question identified the importance of having access to professional development. There is a recognition that one's development as a professional continues past the formal training period and that professional development can support that development.

Findings from Interviews

The interview findings reflect the three questions that underpin this study. The first question, "What are novice early childhood educators' perceptions of their induction experiences in their first year as an early childhood educator?," is answered through the themes identified as "preparedness" and "philosophy." Themes identified for the second and third research questions will be described further on.

Research Question One: What are beginning early childhood educators' perceptions of their induction experiences in their first year as an early childhood educator?

Preparedness

All eleven new early childhood educators spoke about experiences related to preparedness for the work as an early childhood educator. A majority (7 of 11 [64 percent]) described their experience as a first-year early childhood educator as one where they did not feel prepared for the overwhelming workload.

Kim shared her experience in this way: "Well, I was kind of just thrown in there, and I kind of had to teach myself a lot of things that needed to be done." Elizabeth shared her thoughts on how she and her coworker got through the first year: "We kind of just worked through it and figured it out on the way, but looking back I was like 'Wow—so unprepared.'" Connie shared her experience: "It was kind of like I had to just learn what other people did and try my best to do the same." Kathleen discussed the added challenge of being asked to take on a leadership position in her first year of work, which is something that happens regularly due to the high turnover in the field of early childhood education:

> And for me, my biggest challenge was that I was asked to become a supervisor about five or six months after I started working. So, I had to take a leadership role, which was a big challenge. When I was still learning about my role as a beginning educator, I had to kind of think about the more . . . responsibilities I had to take on, so it was kind of difficult.

Sarah said this about her first day on the job: "When I walked in, it was very much 'sink or swim'. It was, 'Here's the room, here's the kids, take care of them.'" Gina portrayed her experience in this way: "You are not introduced to the program much, you don't get to meet the other staff, you have to find your way around." Joel explained the many responsibilities a new educator may be involved in:

> On day two as a new staff I am now opening the centre, which means I am there at 7:30 in the morning and there's a whole lot of responsibilities and everybody coming off of a break is different from what it was before, so I need to have a

different area cleaned up. You not only need to be able to juggle your shift and all of your responsibilities, you also need to know where everybody else is . . . I was very unhappy with how quickly the expectations went right up to full speed.

Despite the fact that most early childhood educators in this study felt unprepared for the work, two new early childhood educators from this same group who spoke of preparedness reported the work with children was rewarding. Speaking of her work, Emma articulated it this way: *"I really enjoy it because there is no such time limit or one single thing that I have to teach. It's just sharing experiences with children. That part I really enjoy working in the field."* Joel highlighted the positive nature of the work, while speaking about the challenge: *"It is incredibly rewarding to work with young children and to bond with families and watch young children grow and be part of that process. On the other hand, it's very difficult to do that hundreds of days in a row."*

Two new early childhood educators (2 of 11 [18 percent]) described their first year as an early childhood educator as being a smooth transition. Alison acknowledged that this was in part due to the fact that her final practicum had taken place at her job site, which meant a great deal of familiarity with the children, families, staff, and program. Alison described her first year this way:

It was fantastic because the transition was very simple, if I can say simple. From going to being a student in practicum and then going into that room and continuing to be an educator in that room . . . with those same people, same senior educator. I knew the executive director already, so as far as that transition went, it made it very easy.

Sophie acknowledged a supportive environment and a familiar philosophy to the one she had learned in school as helping to ensure a smooth transition. She shared, *"I think I was fortunate to have a very supportive environment."* Thus, while most felt unprepared for the workload, a small group experienced smooth transitions, while others found rewards somewhat balanced out difficulty. Philosophy will be discussed next.

Philosophy

Philosophy was something that several (5 of 11 [45 percent]) new early childhood educators raised as an issue in their experience in their first year as an early childhood educator. Each childcare program is run utilizing a particular philosophy of care and education, and this varies from program to program, based on several factors including the type of program and program staff. Early childhood education students learn about a variety of educational philosophies and are encouraged to develop their own personal philosophy of care and education. Graduates of early childhood education post-secondary institutions may find themselves working in a program that has a different philosophy to the one(s) they have been exposed to in their education. Alternately, novice educators may be employed in a program where they do not personally agree with the program philosophy. Several factors may be at play in a situation like this, including a lack of discussion ahead of time about the program philosophy and/or how the program philosophy is carried out on a daily basis. Emma, Sarah, and Kim identified philosophical differences as being issues for them in their workplaces.

In 2010, the government of British Columbia produced *The Early Learning Framework*, which is a document describing the content areas for young children's learning within childcare programs. This was updated in 2021 and now includes an emphasis on Indigenous ways of knowing. A key piece of this document has been the introduction of pedagogical narrations or learning stories, which are essentially stories of what children are learning. Pedagogical narrations involve both photographs and text and are used as a vehicle to communicate with children, families, and educators. Though widely known in the early childhood education community within British Columbia and taught within post-secondary settings, not all early childhood educators use pedagogical narrations, and this is something that Emma came across in her first year of work. Emma shared:

> *I want to try documentation, pedagogical narrations, but some people really strongly disagree with that practice and then I feel like my learning is actually stopped there. I studied something new and I believe that it is important to this field, but then I try to bring that into the field and I am stopped. Like because they have more seniority and they are more experienced, they kind of see me as incompetent and sometimes I feel like I am told, "Hey what are you talking about? That's nonsense. Period. Stop". I feel like there's no faith that I can be. I have to stop myself there. And that's a huge dilemma. Then I just say to myself, "Why am I spending so much time and money and study and can't even use the knowledge?"*

One can see from Emma's comments that contradictions in philosophies among colleagues have led her to question her choices in continuing her education.

Comparing the philosophy of her first job to the various practica she participated in as an early childhood education student, Sarah commented, *"It was a very different philosophy."* Sarah contrasted two different approaches to sharing the program philosophy with staff, using examples from her first and second jobs:

> *Philosophy is a big one. I mean, how much independence do you give your educator when you say, "Alright, here is our parent handbook. Read it through yourself", versus at our centre [Sarah's second job], "This is what we feel we believe". And I think I'm more of a people person, so telling me "That's where you'll find our philosophy is in that binder", but then not giving me prep time to sit down and read it are two different things, too then right?*

Sarah's experience is in contrast to what Sophie encountered in her first job:

> *It [the program] went along with the philosophy that I learned and liked/preferred through our ECE program. I think it was a smooth transition into my employment versus some people may enter a childcare program that isn't what they learned about or is a philosophy that isn't something that fits for them.*

Kim highlighted another issue in early childhood education, where at times one's supervisor is not an early childhood educator, so has a different perspective on the way the work should be done. Kim shared:

> *Another challenge I had was not always having all the support from my supervisor in that. She was gone a lot. She didn't have her ECE, so she didn't spend a lot of time in the classroom, which made it difficult when it came to decision-making. She'd say one thing and I'd know that it would be better to go another way, but she was the supervisor, right? She was the boss.*

As a new educator, Kathleen spoke about the difficulty she encountered due to philosophical differences and a lack of communication about philosophy:

> *I think I had to struggle a lot because of the different philosophies and . . . there is no agreement on philosophy even between—among—the educators who work with . . . in the same room. I wasn't sure what kind of philosophy my supervisor had. My philosophy was kind of emerging and I was learning about my own philosophy, a developing philosophy, but it wasn't obvious. My supervisor's philosophy wasn't clear either. We never talked about that. But she started theme-based curriculum, so I kind of followed.*

As you continue to read through the chapters in Part I, you will see that the content and concepts are interlinked. For example, while this chapter has had a focus on the role of the early childhood educators, the topic of the supervisor came up, as the supervisor has a significant impact on how well new early childhood educators adjust to their new role. More detail and information will be discussed in subsequent chapters, but it will be good to remember that coworkers, supervisors, executive directors, and others have a pivotal role in the adjustment of a new early childhood educator. As you can see from the comments from early childhood educators, there is a lot of wisdom and knowledge coming out of their experiences in adjusting to the new role. In Part II, I will share possible ideas for educator support, based on what educators said was helpful.

3

Adjusting to the Field of Early Childhood Education

Context for the Field of Early Childhood Education

The field of early childhood education is complex, with many facets. In the previous chapter we looked at the role of the early childhood educator, beginning at the program level, and how the educator adjusted to the early childhood education program that they were working in. From there, we looked specifically at adjusting to the new role, from a broader context that included how educators are viewed by society, the support an ECE receives from supervisors, and feelings about the role. In this chapter, we look at the field of early childhood education, beginning with the experiences in the classroom that the educator is involved in. This includes some of the specific tasks that early childhood educators take on from within the new role. Important to recall here is the fact that many new early childhood educators are put into positions of authority, where they may, for example, be the most qualified in the room. This can put undue pressure on the novice educator, who while qualified, still requires ongoing support. From there, we expand the focus to include how early childhood educators are perceived by others in the workplace, the kind of support they are receiving, if any, access to professional development, and knowledge of professional associations, which are often places of support.

Adjustment to the Early Childhood Education Classroom

As seen in Table 3.0, 17–43 percent of new early childhood educators in this survey reported they did not get the help they needed. The average from this was 30 percent. While 22 percent of new educators reported receiving more than what they needed with respect to evaluating children's progress, 40 percent of

Table 3.0 Adjustment to Early Childhood Education Classroom Scale—What Was Received

Question	Received Less	Received What Was Needed	Received More
Becoming acquainted with the contents of the classroom	34%	35%	31%
Dealing with the lack of equipment	35%	32.5%	32.5%
Implementing the program philosophy in the classroom	27%	42%	31%
Knowing how the classroom I am working in fits in with the total ECE program	22%	52%	26%
Dealing with the physical organization of the room	17%	37%	46%
Dealing with the guidance related to children's behavior	27%	36%	36%
Evaluating children's progress	40%	38%	22%
Preparing reports	32%	42%	26%
Becoming acquainted with the children I work with and their backgrounds	28%	40%	32%
Being given opportunities to observe experienced educators at work	34%	36%	30%
Having a procedure available which encourages me to discuss problems caused by my inexperience	39%	25%	36%
Being given a workload which reflects my training and lack of experience	34%	41%	25%
Being given opportunities to grow professionally through the provision of in-service programs	38%	35%	27%
Having a variety of strategies to deal with the different needs of the children	34%	34%	32%
Organizing time to deal with matters such as program planning, report writing, and other clerical tasks	43%	34%	23%
Communicating with family members about the child's day	26%	38%	36%
Coordinating parent volunteers	19%	64%	17%
Preparing for parent conferences/meetings and "meet the teacher" nights	19%	62%	19%
Knowing how to deal with health needs or physical restrictions of children	29%	44%	27%
Locating or ordering supplies	26%	44%	30%
Lack of similarity between theory or practice	32%	49%	19%

participants reported receiving less than what they needed. As with the previous scale, it is interesting to note that 46 percent of early childhood educators reported receiving more than what they needed in the area of dealing with the physical organization of the room, while 17 percent reported receiving less than needed. When asked about "being given a workload which reflects my training and lack of experience" the responses were varied, with 34 percent receiving less than needed, 41 percent receiving what was needed, and 25 percent receiving more than was needed. While the majority (49 percent) of new early childhood educators received what they needed with regard to the "lack of similarity between theory and practice," 32 percent reported receiving less than what was needed. Of those who responded by saying they received less than what was needed, 25 percent reported receiving no support and 35 percent reported receiving little support with regard to the lack of similarity between theory and practice.

When asked if they had anything else to share regarding other perceived needs related to the adjustment to the early childhood classroom, eighteen new early childhood educators brought up the following aspects: program philosophy, communication with families, licensing requirements, and regular on-site professional development. Three of the educators identified themselves as having to figure things out on their own, without the support of fellow educators. Here are some of the quotations:

- *Need skills of communication with families;*
- *Offer regular professional development on site; and*
- *Dealing with licensing was a learning experience in my first year. I had to do a lot of research online to answer most of my questions.*

The educators who shared the open-ended questions indicated their formal schooling was not enough. They continued to need support on the jobsite. New early childhood educators have learning needs once on the job.

Adjustment to the Field of Early Childhood Education

Individual responses from beginning early childhood educators were tallied to determine the number of educators who received less than what they needed, exactly what they needed, and more than what they needed with regard to adjusting to the field of early childhood education, and this is displayed in Table 3.1.

As seen in Table 3.1, 29–51 percent of early childhood educators in this survey reported they did not get the help they needed. The average from this was

Table 3.1 Field of Early Childhood Education Scale—What Was Received

Question	Received Less	Received What Was Needed	Received More
Having confidence in my role as an ECE	32%	30%	38%
Feeling comfortable interacting with all program staff	29%	36%	35%
Feeling that the parents recognize me as a competent educator	31%	33%	36%
Feeling that the executive director or supervisor recognizes me as a competent educator	30%	34%	36%
Becoming knowledgeable about the services offered by the ECEBC associations (provincial or local)	51%	29%	20%
Becoming an active member of the ECEBC local association	42%	43%	15%
Becoming an active member of the ECEBC provincial association	42%	43%	15%
Having access to professional development resources	33.33%	33.34%	33.33%
Having access to workshops, conferences, etc.	33%	32%	35%

36 percent. While 20 percent of participants reported receiving more than what they needed with respect to "becoming knowledgeable about the services offered by the ECEBC associations," 51 percent of participants reported receiving less than what they needed. Additionally, while 35 percent reported receiving more than what they needed regarding "having access to workshops, conferences, etc.," 33 percent received less than what they needed.

Open-Ended Questions

When asked to share other perceived needs relating to the adjustment to the field of early childhood education, thirteen new early childhood educators shared ideas regarding having professional development that is accessible, in terms of time and money, practice-based workshops, learning about community resources, and being part of ECEBC, the provincial association representing early childhood educators. Some of the comments shared are:

- *There used to be over time allowed for attending workshops, now it is on your own time;*

- *Workshops need to focus on the practical aspects of dealing with children, rather than the theoretical;*
- *Workshops and conferences are way too expensive for the amount of pay that most educators receive which makes them inaccessible by those who need them; and*
- *Belonging to ECEBC should be included in all provincial ECE training programs.*

New early childhood educators who answered this open-ended question talked about the importance of having accessible professional development in order to remain current in the field. Given the nature of the early childhood education field where access to professional development is inconsistent, it makes sense that new educators identified this as a concern. Additionally, sometimes professional development is available in larger communities but may not be accessible in an educator's own community, making professional development even more costly as it includes travel and accommodation.

Additional Open-Ended Questions

In the third and final open-ended question, new early childhood educators were asked, "Is there anything else you would like to share about your experiences as a beginning early childhood educator?" Thirty-six new educators responded, sharing thoughts on the positive and negative aspects of the job of an early childhood educator, which speak to the adjustment to the field of early childhood education.

Challenging Work

The majority (9) of the new early childhood educators wrote about the challenges in early childhood education work. Here are two of the comments:

- *I got satisfaction more coming from the response of the children, and the parents/families then the feedback and support of other program staff or supervisor. However, this is also the main motive or passion for me to be an ECE; and*
- *There have been so many times in my first year that I had to think to myself, wow, this was not covered in ECE. For example, dealing with unhappy*

parents, progress reports for the children, licensing regulations, significant family issues, even how to properly change a diaper. I think that I did however feel confident in my abilities to problem solve situations from the experiences I did get in the ECE program. The first year is by far the hardest year for any ECE!

The early childhood education context is one that can be challenging due to issues discussed in Chapter 1: high turnover of staff, first year characterized as "survival," burnout, directors without increased education, and lack of government funding for early learning programs.

As the wage of early childhood educators in British Columbia (and elsewhere) is considered low, it was not surprising to see comments regarding this challenge:

- *I like my job, and I see the importance of it. But the pay and benefits does not reflect the importance of my position, rather it demeans my importance and makes me want to switch job fields. Pay is a big issue in the Early Childhood Field;*
- *As I knew ahead of time, the wages are significantly too low; and*
- *This is a severely overworked and underpaid career. The stress and responsibility are also grossly disproportionate to the low centre morale and this actually overcomes the great feeling of satisfaction one gets from educating children through play.*

Positive Aspects of the Work

Some new early childhood educators (7) wrote about positive aspects of the work that they found to be either rewarding and/or helpful to them in the first year of work:

- *For a beginning educator, having a mentor is very helpful. New graduates from the ECE program need lots of support in learning about various philosophy and generating their own philosophy and how to put them into practice on a daily basis;*
- *Working in a centre that supports personal philosophy is VERY important!; and*
- *It has been the most difficult work experience in some ways, but the reward out weigh the other stuff!!! It is hard work, but I learned to play more and I am reaping the benefits! Happy children makes me happy too!!!.*

Job Satisfaction

Table 3.2 demonstrates the responses from new early childhood educators on their current job satisfaction. By far, most educators indicated they are satisfied with their work as an early childhood educator. When asked to rate their agreement on the following statement, "I get a lot of satisfaction out of my work as an early childhood educator," 89 percent of beginning early childhood educators in this study agreed or strongly agreed with the statement. When asked if they would choose early childhood education again if they were starting out and could choose their life's work, 68 percent of the participants reported

Table 3.2 Teacher Job Satisfaction in Individual Items (N = 62)

Job Satisfaction Items	Strongly Disagree %	Disagree %	Neutral %	Agree %	Strongly Agree %
Overall I feel that the early childhood educator training I went through did a good job preparing me for the work of an early childhood educator	1.6	8.06	11.29	46.77	32.36
Early childhood education was my first career choice	8.06	29.03	20.97	19.35	22.58
I wish I had not chosen the field of early childhood education	58.06	19.35	16.13	4.84	1.61
As an early childhood educator, I feel that I am well respected and appreciated	8.06	19.35	30.65	29.03	12.90
The morale of early childhood educators at my center is high	3.23	14.52	22.58	35.48	24.19
I plan to leave the early childhood education field within five years	33.87	25.81	17.74	16.13	6.45
My current profession is a lifelong choice	14.52	8.06	24.19	25.81	27.42
I only chose early childhood education because I had no other choice	51.61	38.71	6.45	3.23	0
If I were just starting out and could choose my life's work all over again, I would choose early childhood education	3.23	9.68	19.35	37.10	30.65
I get a lot of satisfaction out of my work as an early childhood educator	0	0	11.29	41.94	46.77

that they would. Moreover, 90 percent of beginning early childhood educators disagreed or strongly disagreed with the statement, "I only chose early childhood education because I had no other options." Seventy-nine percent of beginning early childhood educators indicated they felt the early childhood educator training they received prepared them for their jobs.

A small number of beginning early childhood educators, however, wished that they had not chosen teaching (6.5 percent). Additionally, while 60 percent of beginning early childhood educators disagreed or strongly disagreed with the statement, "I plan to leave the early childhood education field within five years," 23 percent agreed or strongly agreed with the statement, and 17 percent indicated a neutral response. Furthermore, while 53 percent agreed that early childhood education is a lifelong choice, 24 percent remained neutral, and 23 percent disagreed. Regarding the question of the morale of early childhood educators, 60 percent indicated a high morale at their current workplace, while 23 percent remained neutral, and 18 percent indicated morale is not high. Interestingly, 42 percent of educators in this study indicated they feel respected and appreciated as an early childhood educator, but 31 percent remained neutral, and 27 percent indicated they do not feel respected and appreciated.

Although the work of an educator is challenging at times, new early childhood educators have identified specific strategies and approaches that can be helpful. Knowing that one is supported through a mentor or through a staff group that holds to the same philosophy can encourage a new educator through the challenging times. Additionally, it can be helpful to recognize that even in the midst of difficulty, positive work is being done. In the next chapter, the focus is on supervisory practices.

4

Supervisory Practices

Context for Supervisory Practices

The role of the supervisor is a critical one as they are the person who sets the tone in the room. This role is one that impacts children, families, and educators alike, and for the purposes of this book, the new early childhood educator. As we saw from the introductory chapters, new early childhood educators are developing their professional identity, and it takes time and support. Beginning educators can also deal with imposter syndrome, where they wonder if they have what it takes to be an effective educator. An experienced, knowledgeable, and compassionate supervisor will understand this and will offer reassurance, support, and encouragement. This also requires that supervisors (1) know how to support beginning early childhood educators and (2) have time to support new early childhood educators. Within the fast-paced early learning environment of many early learning centers, this is not always possible. Add to this, that some supervisors are in a new leadership role themselves and may not have the support they need, and you have an interesting situation, one that, unfortunately, is not altogether uncommon.

Adjustment to Supervisory Practices

Table 4.0 provides a visual demonstration of the individual responses related to what was received in adjusting to supervisory practices. When asked about receiving "one-on-one discussions with my primary supervisor to address my goals, concerns, difficulties, etc.," 25 percent of beginning early childhood educators reported receiving more than what they needed, while 41 percent reported receiving less than what they needed. As with previous scales, further analysis took place involving actual counts of those who reported receiving nothing or little in this area. Again, it is important to note that beginning

Table 4.0 Adjustment to Supervisory Practices—What Was Received (*N* = 63)

Question	Received Less	Received What Was Needed	Received More
Primary Supervisor (P.S.) came to my classroom to evaluate me	29%	49%	22%
P.S. visited my classroom to discuss programming and/or provide advice	35%	41%	24%
Regular "drop ins" by my P.S. to help me develop my professional competence	30%	52%	18%
One-on-one discussions with my P.S. to address my goals, concerns, difficulties, etc.	41%	34%	25%
Informal discussions or unscheduled meetings with my P.S. resulting in professional or social discussions	32%	44%	24%

early childhood educators who indicated they received nothing or little did not necessarily want more than they received. In this scale, when individual responses were tallied, 52–56 percent of beginning early childhood educators reported they received nothing or little with regard to the support received. Thirty-two percent of beginning early childhood educators reported they received no visit for evaluation and 22 percent reported receiving little in this area. Therefore, 54 percent of new early childhood educators in this study reported receiving no or little support regarding a classroom evaluation. Twenty-four percent of beginning early childhood educators reported receiving nothing receiving nothing when it came to one-on-one discussions with their primary supervisor to address their goals, concerns, difficulties, and so on. A further 29 percent reported receiving little, for a total of 52 percent of beginning early childhood educators receiving no or little support in this area. Based on individual responses of what was needed and what was received, between 29 percent and 41 percent of beginning early childhood educators in this study indicated they did not receive the support they needed in adjusting to supervisory practices.

Beginning early childhood educators were invited to respond in an open-ended manner regarding other perceived needs relating to supervisory practices by the primary supervisor, and thirteen shared their thoughts. New educators discussed the importance of communication among staff, teamwork, the ways supervisors can be helpful, and the inherent conflicts that can exist between coworkers:

- *Primary supervisor is helpful at times, but really loves themes and cookie-cutter art, while I believe in open-ended activities. The primary supervisor*

does not see the merit in those activities. So I do what I can to help my team put up parent pleasing art, but I also document the children in other areas of their significant learning;
- Having a regular meeting to hear from the beginning educator as well as other educators in the room would be helpful to learn about each other's philosophy, practices, and strategies (e.g. ways to guide children with behavior challenges) and discuss some possible emerging themes from children's interests (programming), etc.;
- To spend more time in the program to see what was actually going on, to evaluate staff, to help give constructive criticism.

The comments from participants make sense given this is a field where educators are not guaranteed regular staff meetings or shared planning time. The early childhood educators who took part in this portion of the scale clearly want time to plan and prepare the learning environment and time to discuss the issues related to dealing with conflicts such as differences in program philosophy.

Adjustment to Administrative Practices

As Table 4.1 demonstrates, when beginning early childhood educators were asked to indicate what level of support was received with regard to the statement, "My executive director or supervisor's year end evaluation/report was fair," 19 percent reported receiving less than what was needed, 55 percent reported receiving what was needed, and 26 percent reported receiving more than what was needed. Further analysis took place involving actual counts of those who reported receiving nothing or little in this area. Keeping in mind that participants could have indicated they received more than what they needed, yet received little, the results were: 39 percent of new early childhood educators reported receiving nothing and 15 percent reported receiving little. Therefore, 53 percent of new early childhood educators reported they received nothing or little with regard to a year-end evaluation. When asked to indicate what level of support was received with regard to this statement, "My work is appreciated and commended by my executive director or supervisor," 31 percent reported receiving less than what was needed, 38 percent reported receiving what was needed, and 31 percent reported receiving more than what was needed.

Based on individual responses from beginning early childhood educators on what was needed and what was received, between 19 percent and 31 percent of

Table 4.1 Adjustment to Administrative Practices—What Was Received (*N* = 62)

Question	Received Less	Received What Was Needed	Received More
The executive director (ED) or supervisor (Sup) supports my classroom decisions	24%	44%	32%
The ED or Sup communicates directly with me about his/her evaluation of the effort I am making	29%	40%	31%
My ED or Sup has a reasonable understanding of the problems connected with my current position	29%	40%	31%
I communicate openly and without hesitation with my ED or Sup	26%	37%	37%
My ED or Sup shows an interest in me and in my problems	26%	43%	31%
My work is appreciated and commended by my ED or Sup	31%	35%	34%
My ED or Sup promotes a sense of belonging among the educators in our program	31%	38%	31%
My ED or Sup's year-end evaluation/report was fair	19%	55%	26%

beginning early childhood educators indicated they did not receive the support they needed in adjusting to supervisory practices.

Open-Ended Questions

Beginning early childhood educators were given the opportunity to add additional comments regarding other perceived needs relating to supportive administrative practices. Nine new educators shared ideas related to needing feedback from supervisors (4), the skills of supervisors (4), and having time to observe (1):

- *There was no evaluation on educators' performance;*
- *Being at the site more often to offer assistance with problem solving; and*
- *Our director tends to have a very hands-off approach to the happiness of her staff and requires us to solve issues internally, which is fine for small matters, but sometimes we need conflict resolution from a higher source, which she is not comfortable with.*

Interestingly, one new early childhood educator acknowledged, "this questionnaire is a little difficult for me to answer fairly because my new Senior Educator [supervisor] is great and my past one was horrible, so I just marked moderate all the way down."

Comments from beginning early childhood educators about the lack of evaluation on their own performance fit as there are no formal structures in place to mandate evaluation of early childhood educators. New educators also raised the issue of additional skill and training for supervisors, and this resonates well with the current early childhood education context in British Columbia where supervisors are elevated to leadership positions quickly and do not necessarily have additional training or leadership skills.

Findings from Interviews

The interview findings reflect the three overall questions that underpin this study. The first question, "What are novice early childhood educators' perceptions of their induction experiences in their first year as an early childhood educator?," was shared in Chapter 2. The second question, "What, if any, kind(s) of induction support do novice early childhood educators receive in their first year and how effective are these in supporting novice early childhood educators' development of professional capacity?," is answered here, through the following aspects: level of support received, kinds of support received, participation in induction activities, types of induction activities offered, who one would go to for support, and what else was helpful in the induction year. Themes were identified for each aspect and will be outlined individually below. The third research question will be addressed in the next chapter.

Research Question Two: What, if any, kind(s) of induction support do novice early childhood educators receive in their first year and how effective are these in supporting novice early childhood educators' development of Professional capacity?

Lack of Support

While beginning early childhood educators encounter a wide variety of experiences in their first year, a majority (7 of 11 [64 percent]) of the new educators indicated that they did not receive the support they needed in their first year of work.

Beginning early childhood educators who were interviewed in this study were asked if they felt they received the support they needed in their first year of work. Most (64 percent) revealed they did not receive the support required. Joel shared, "*There weren't staff right there who I could ask for help, assistance or to remind me of something that needed to be done. It was very much hit the ground running, on your own.*" Sarah, who acknowledged that despite doing well in school, still needed support, stated:

> *I had just graduated when I walked into this building and it was sort of like, "Yeah, we know you're great. Go to town". And you're like, Ah, I still need support, like I still need support. I may be right out of grad school and I may have done really well as far as my program and my grades and my practicum, and my instructors all may say that I am a wonderful educator, great. But you know I still need someone to say to me, "Sarah, here we like to do it this way or Sarah, if you are interested, there's these things out there". Don't think I don't I don't need a workshop, just because I just finished school.*

Like Sarah, Anna too realized she still needed support as she did not know as much as an experienced educator: "*We don't know all the things that a ten-year ECE knows.... It would be nice if they could remind me of things or have constructive criticism instead of it just being criticism.*" Though she received support from the supervisor, Connie was hoping for more from others in her job site: "*But I definitely was looking for more support from the owner and administrator, which I found lacking, and so that was really challenging too.*" Elizabeth who was working with another beginning early childhood educator, reported: "*No, I don't think I received the full amount of support that we needed.*" When asked why she thought this, Elizabeth explained it this way:

> *Because it wasn't really there, because of the feeling that you don't want to bug somebody else and you don't want to take them out of their job or their . . . there was no time I felt that you could sit down with someone and say "Hey, I'm dealing with this situation. What are some good options that I can do? How can I rectify this situation?"*

A small number (2 of 11 [18 percent]) of beginning early childhood educators shared the view that they did receive the support they needed; however, one new educator from this group spoke about receiving the support only from one particular job site, but not the other ones she had been involved in. Gina described her experience of receiving support this way:

> *You see, when you joined the company, you had a couple of days' introduction to the company itself and to its policy and to its procedures, and you met the director at that time too. . . . That made a big difference. You feel you belonged there.*

Alison shared the support she felt when it came to implementing curriculum she was interested in: "*I am always eager to keep on learning and extending what I am doing . . . and as far as that goes, my senior educator and my executive director and my whole team was very, very much encouraging and always giving feedback, always really, really supportive in terms of me continuing my education amongst the room.*"

A slightly larger number of beginning early childhood educators (3 of 11 [27 percent]) did not answer definitively in the affirmative or the negative citing an inconsistent level of support due to issues such as the high turnover of staff and the subsequent inconsistency in support. In this excerpt from Kathleen, the issue of new educators being elevated to positions of leadership due to high turnover is highlighted: "*I had a room supervisor and she just got hired, just like me, so she was a new educator as well. . . . She was learning about that too, like about the program, so we were both learning about the program.*" Sophie's response also emphasizes the issue of the high turnover of staff in childcare programs, while discussing the possible confusion this can bring for new early childhood educators:

> *I feel I've had incredible amounts of support at different periods, not consistently. So I think that consistent support . . . which also comes with consistent staffing. As we know, there is high turnover in ECE, so I think if you entered into a program that was staffed with supportive, knowledgeable, educated staff, and that group stayed together for a certain duration of time, then I would feel that continuity of support. Whereas, I've had experiences with that but it hasn't been continuous, so in one way I've got to see many different educators' approaches, but in another way it just confuses things, right? Because then you don't have a confident approach, it's more of a "maybe", whereas I think other people who have worked with a confident supervisor or team leader throughout, it's a little bit easier for them to know "This is what you can do if you need a care plan; this is what you can do if you have an accident; this is where you can go . . .", and it's a bit of a more clear laid out plan, whereas now, if something comes up, it's still like "Okay, I gotta think about this. What shall we do here?" because I've seen so many different ways.*

Finding 2. The Research Question of what kinds of support novice early childhood educators receive is answered through the themes of "support from jobsite" and "support from community."

Support from Jobsite

Prior to inquiring about specific induction support, new early childhood educators were asked to describe the kinds of support they received in their first year of work as an early childhood educator. A majority of beginning early childhood educators (9 of 11 [82 percent]) reported receiving support from their jobsite. Of this group, most (7 of 9 [78 percent]) were supported by their coworkers. Unlike school teachers, who often work individually in separate classrooms, early childhood educators often work in teams, with, for example, three educators and twenty-four children. Emma discussed the support she received in dealing with the challenges of communicating when there are cultural differences:

> How can I put this? Working with other people is really important, like how to communicate and stuff like that. It was hard for me to understand other people's ways because I am in a new country and I speak English as a second language and the cultural differences and everything. I think my worksite was really supportive for me to go through that difficulty. I shouldn't say difficulty, but it's a difference. It's different experience than I had back home, so going through that, you know, how to deal with conflict, how to talk to other people, what is active listening, stuff like that was really new to me and my workplace was really supportive to help me to understand the differences between my culture and this new culture.

In talking about her second job, where she did receive the support she needed, Sarah says this:

Though she did not receive the level of support she needed, Elizabeth was able to get some support from a coworker who was on a leave at the time:

> I didn't really know where to go for support. I knew that I could go to my boss or the other co-workers that I worked with, if we had any questions, but beyond that it was hard to contact ECEBC [Early Childhood Educators of British Columbia] or the CCRR [Child Care Resources and Referral]. I haven't done that before so I was very unfamiliar with how to get the support from other people, because I found that I wouldn't want to put my boss out of her way saying, "Hey, I have a question for you again" or my co-workers. It was nice because I was covering someone on leave, so I would call her all the time and be like, "This just happened, what do we do here?" . . . So there was support, but it wasn't like . . . it wasn't easy to find.

Sophie described the close working relationship she had with one of her coworkers:

> I've had the privilege to work with one early childhood educator who has been in the field for many years and is passionate about it and really enjoys talking

about the different children and about programming and stuff like that. She really enjoys conversations around that, so it helped me to continually think about the practice and what we were doing and why we were doing it versus just putting out a new activity or a new toy for a child, or planning something—there was always the "why", and talking about each individual child and how we could support this child more and things like that. So, I think she was very helpful.

Support from the Community

Several of the beginning early childhood educators (4 of 11 [36 percent]) described support they received from the community. This took several forms, including support from one's own family, support from early childhood education friends, post-secondary instructors, and professional development opportunities offered in the early childhood education community. Alison discussed the difference her family support made to her:

I come from a very large, huge, stable, loud family, and they're interested in what I do, which is nice. It's easy because, I have friends however, who think its babysitting. So that's hard to take. That was very hard to take at the beginning. Very hard to take because you work so hard to get your diploma, you do all this like researching and presentations, and you have such a confidence about what you are doing and then someone looks at you and says, "What do you do, play for a living?" . . . But having your family back you up. We always have family dinners and I blabber about what I'm doing at work with the children and they are asking. They're so interested and amazed at what children are doing and all of what we do extra with our families, and how much effort we put in our day. They're like, "That's daycare?" They can't believe it, right?

Anna found she received support from friends who were early childhood educators, people she had been in school with. In speaking about who she received support from she shared: "*Definitely support from other ECEs. . . . I did keep in contact with some ECE students, like on Facebook.*" Often early childhood education programs in post-secondary institutions have email list serves of former and current students that are used to share information on community news such as job postings and professional development opportunities. Alison found this source of support from her former post-secondary instructor to be helpful: "*The email list from my instructor is a huge support. Just with job opportunities, ECEBC information, that kind of stuff. That I would think of as being a support, definitely."* Sarah echoed the importance of sharing information on professional development and/or how to get involved with ECEBC, the provincial organization for early childhood educators in British Columbia, something that occurred at her second jobsite:

> *Those kinds of support where you have the support of your team that you are working with for whatever reason, how to get to ECEBC, I had huge support because I was still in school, when I went to ECEBC. . . . But, if it's never talked about in your workplace, you may never consider going. Whether it be to a Saturday workshop or whether it be to a huge conference. If your workplace is not getting that information to you and saying, "You gonna come? Are you gonna go?" Or "Do you need your hours for your certification?" Anything like that, that's how they can support beginning ECE's.*

Inconsistent Induction Support

Beginning early childhood educators were asked if they received induction support such as mentoring, feedback, observations on practice, and professional development in their first year. While many (5 of 11 [45 percent]) said they did not receive this kind of support, some (4 of 11 [36 percent]) said they did receive induction support, and others (2 of 11 [18 percent]) said they did so to a degree, but that it was not enough and/or it was not offered to the novice but instead initiated by the novice early childhood educator themselves. Sarah shared this when asked if she had received induction support: "*No feedback, no professional development. If they were observing me, I wasn't aware of it and they never said anything negative or positive.*" Emma who identified herself as one who had received induction support, talked about receiving feedback through an evaluation:

> *Every year we have a personal evaluation between the supervisor and myself and that evaluation will go to the director. . . . In order to do the evaluation, I have to show on the forms that I have my goals and everything. And I have to evaluate myself first and then bring that to my supervisor. . . . And then she will give me feedback. And this is not just a one day thing. Having a meeting is just a one day thing. . . . Daily, she knows what I like to do, we often have conversations based on the knowledge that we share.*

Alison described her experience of wanting to hear her supervisor's feedback: "And I just love feedback and I just wanted to know what I was doing that was good and okay, and professional enough, and if I was doing enough. And if I wasn't doing enough, how could I change that?" Connie talked about how she was the one to initiate induction activities such as feedback and observation:

> I would say it was more of my own doing. Like feedback would be because I asked for it, not because there was a set time when, for example, the head educator or whoever would sit down and give me feedback on my performance or anything like that. And the same thing with observation and things like that. I never had the time given to me to do that. I just did it, kind of like on the go, how I said before, so I mean those were processes that I went through but it was more on my own doing rather than something that was a standard of the centre where I worked, as a part of a new employee.

Joel, who did identify himself as experiencing induction activities to a degree, received informal mentoring for the first couple of months on the job.

Induction Activities

Of the beginning early childhood educators who did take part in induction activities (4 of 11), all received mentoring, feedback, and professional development. In British Columbia, where there are no standards or specific programs to support beginning early childhood educators, the mentoring that the participants experienced was on an informal basis. Joel had this to say about his mentor: *"She was somebody, the one person I absolutely felt comfortable going to, to ask any question, even if it was making me look like I had left something out or I had done something wrong. She was absolutely the one person on staff that I could talk to."* When asked if his mentor had been assigned, Joel had this to say:

> Oh absolutely not. Not assigned at all . . . it was just the person that I felt closest to . . . she was the one I felt comfortable with, to go to, and the woman who actually, the one staff that actually took an interest in me, the one person who seemed to understand how difficult everything was and that there was a certain level of support needed and obviously and it was apparently up to her to provide that support, I'm assuming.

Sophie discussed the process of how she came to have a mentor:

> Mentoring maybe not, maybe it wasn't purposeful, but I did find a mentor . . . just connecting with somebody who I liked a lot of their practice. Of course, I'm an individual person and I educated myself but I liked a lot of their practice and so I found myself observing that person and communicating with her a lot, and so I think that she has mentored me.

Workplace Support

When beginning early childhood educators were asked what else has been helpful to them in their first year as an early childhood educator, the majority (6 of 11 [55 percent]) reported that workplace examples were helpful. Some (5 of 11 [45 percent]) said preservice experiences were helpful, and a couple (2 of 11 [18 percent]) described early childhood education community experiences as being helpful. Two of the new educators spoke about the importance of being valued in the workplace. Speaking about her second job, Sarah reported:

> *They've also been very supportive of me as an educator and not looking at me as a new educator. Not that my old job didn't. I mean honestly, they gave me all the independence in the world, but this team is coming to me and saying, "What's your opinion?", "How do you feel about?"... They're not directing me, they're including me, and therefore giving me value in my skills by making me feel like an equal member of their team.*

Emma spoke about the importance of feeling valued:

> *Here, like for example, my director of the program tells everyone she doesn't hire anybody as an assistant. There are no assistants. Many educators working in one centre, but nobody is an assistant, even if you are new to the centre. That kind of reminder supports me as mentally.... If I hear director's voice, I can make a decision as an early childhood educator, with my little experience and knowledge. Even a little experience is countable.*

Joel indicated that observing other educators had been the most helpful to him. In this quotation, he shares an example from an observation he gleaned from visiting another center:

> *The one time I got to go to another centre after not being overwhelmed, being the new person on the job and being fairly comfortable with my position was eager to go ... being able to go in and just have fun with them [the children]. Then calmly observe the centre, picking up on different things that other people did, just in terms of, all across the spectrum, just walking in and hearing somebody getting ready to go outside while I am taking my jacket off and they might say a couple of lines: "Alright, I've put a few things around the, around the play yard, you know, let's go on a different", whatever items that he hid, going down the list of them, and while I am taking my jacket off, I'm thinking, "Ah, I haven't done a little treasure hunt for so long. That would be a great idea".*

The result for Joel was a renewed sense of what was possible with regard to outdoor programming.

Preservice Experiences

Regarding the helpfulness of preservice experiences, Alison spoke about practicum and coursework:

> *Definitely practicum was helpful. The first year I find group time was a challenge because of just like 30 minutes every day for five days. It was a huge, but I think without that course [curriculum development], I'd be—screwed. I had that binder [of resources] in my group time basket forever, like forever and like the other educators were borrowing my binder all the time.*

Anna found it helpful to refer back to textbooks used in school: "*Keeping some of my old textbooks, for sure. I've kept the child guidance textbook and I kept that really nice textbook by Deb Curtis, all the early childhood environments—those were very good resources that I held onto.*"

Early Childhood Education Community Experiences

Beginning early childhood educators found experiences in the early childhood education community to be helpful. These included professional development, early childhood educators who were friends, and post-secondary instructors. Sophie spoke about the added benefit of networking when taking part in professional development in the community:

> *I think the professional development has been very helpful because it also gets you out in the community and to meet other individuals. Because my experiences have been fairly limited to the one childcare centre, I haven't had the opportunity to meet with people in the community, other educators in the community, so I've enjoyed the professional development for that reason, for networking.*

Connie indicated she found support in early childhood educators who were friends of hers:

> *I think having connections with some of the other students still, from my program at the university. We definitely didn't get the chance to talk as much as we did when we were seeing each other every day in the program, but there was a couple of people that I still kept in touch with and saw every now and then, and we were able to kind of share our different experiences and things like that.*

Sarah mentioned the following community experiences that were helpful to her: "*Anything that can support a new ECE coming into the field in the form of that, be that resources from the CCRR [Child Care Resource and Referral], from other classmates, from instructors or even the fact that one of the instructors sends out job postings.*"

Support from Coworkers

When participants were asked to whom they would go now for support, the majority (9 of 11 [82 percent]) reported they would go to people in their workplace. In addition, some (3 of 11 [27 percent]) said they would go to people in the early childhood education community for support. One participant indicated she had no one she could go to for support. Joel reported he would speak to his coworkers: "*I would really go back to the three staff that I worked with.*" Elizabeth, who works on her own, has developed her own support network:

> *I go to lots of people. I network now on Facebook with a lot of people I graduated with. We kind of all kept in touch. I also talk to a former sponsor educator a lot too. She's been a really good support for me. I talk to my other co-workers. I have called the CCRR [Child Care Resources and Referral] before and said "Hey, this happened, what do I do and how do I deal with it?" I also have a good relationship with licensing and I talk to my licensing officer about stuff. So, now I feel I know where I can go for help.*

When asked to whom she might go for support, Gina replied, "*I have no-one. To be honest, I have no-one.*"

Unpredictable Future

When asked if they saw themselves continuing in the early childhood education field in the future, many beginning early childhood educators (5 of 11 [45 percent]) reported they would stay in the field. Some (3 of 11 [27 percent]) indicated they did not see themselves continuing in the field and the same number (3 of 11 [27 percent]) shared they were unsure. Sarah responded in the affirmative, saying she sees herself staying in the early childhood education field: "*Yes, very much so. . . . I think professional development is the only way to stay active in the field, to meet other educators, to connect with other educators and yeah, that's why I got into it. I see a huge future for it.*" Several of the participants brought up the issue of wage, citing that as a reason for leaving the field. Alison shared:

> *If we made a living you know, you felt like you were supporting yourself, you could support someone else, a dependent on you? That would make all the difference, but like if something happened to my partner and I had a child, I could not, I know people do, but it's not, it would be very difficult to support yourself and another person.*

Joel said he was unsure about his staying in the field:

> *I really can't say. Ah, the options are very limited in terms of, I would have to choose, essentially a supervisor position, I think makes $22 an hour and that's as high as you can go until you come off the floor and start doing administrative work and I'm not interested in doing administrative work. I really enjoy working with young children, so would I be able to own a home and drive a car on $22? It is a very difficult prospect.*

Joel added a further reason for the high turnover:

> *I think in my opinion the predominant reason why there is such rampant turnover in the field, there is simply, the people I have talked to have, it's just "too much" is a word they often use to describe, it's just burned them out.*

The third overall research question, "What, if any, forms of induction or novice professional development would novice early childhood educators like to take part in, and why?," is answered through the themes identified as "support for novice early childhood educators," "supportive work environment," "support from early childhood education community," and "support for experienced early childhood educators." This will be shared in the next chapter on "Induction Support."

5

Induction Support

Context for Induction Support

As mentioned previously, induction refers to both the time period when an early childhood educator is first in the field, usually the first year, and specific induction activities such as mentoring, feedback, observations, and professional development (Winstead Fry, 2010; Aitken et al., 2008). Induction is not always a word that is associated with early childhood educators, and in some contexts, there is more familiarity with the term among teachers within the school system. Many of the educators I have met have felt drawn to the concept of induction, as well as what it means. When put into practice, early childhood educators are given timely support and mentorship that can help them as they transition into their new role. Unfortunately, for many, this experience is not common, and instead, new early childhood educators often find themselves ushered into a new position without adequate support. In some cases, there is added pressure and expectation placed upon them as they may be the only fully qualified educator in the room and/or the most qualified.

Induction-Related Questions

Within the survey for new early childhood educators, there were specific questions related to induction. These questions have been identified, and individual responses to what was received were computed. In Table 5.0, the percentages received for feedback, observations, professional development, and mentoring are visually represented. Other induction-related activities are shown in Table 5.1. The questions were chosen from across the entire questionnaire. The criterion was that the question must relate to one of the induction activities. Tables 5.2 and 5.3 also visually demonstrate the percentage of participants

Table 5.0 Percentage of Feedback, Observations, Professional Development, and Mentoring Received

Feedback	Received Less Than Needed	Received What Was Needed	Received More Than Needed	Received Nothing	Received Little	Total None/Little
The ED or Sup communicates directly with me about his/her evaluation of the effort I am making	29%	40%	31%	16%	31%	47%
P.S. came to my classroom to evaluate me	29%	49%	22%	32%	22%	54%
My ED or Sup's year-end evaluation/report was fair	19%	55%	26%	39%	15%	53%
Observations	Received Less Than Needed	Received What Was Needed	Received More Than Needed	Received Nothing	Received Little	Total None/Little
Being given opportunities to observe experienced educators at work	34%	36%	30%	18%	27%	45%
Professional Development	Received Less Than Needed	Received What Was Needed	Received More Than Needed	Received Nothing	Received Little	Total None/Little
Being given opportunities to grow professionally through the provision of in-service programs	38%	35%	27%	22%	25%	47%
Having access to professional development resources	33.33%	33.33%	33.33%	17%	26%	46%
Having access to workshops, conferences, etc.	33%	32%	35%	19%	19%	39%
Mentoring	Received Less Than Needed	Received What Was Needed	Received More Than Needed	Received Nothing	Received Little	Total None/Little
Forming a connection with an experienced ECE	25%	36%	24%	17%	19%	37%
P.S. visited my classroom to discuss programming and/or provided advice	35%	41%	24%	21%	35%	56%

Regular "drop-ins" by my P.S. to help me develop my professional competence	30%	52%	18%	21%	35%	56%
One-on-one discussions with P.S. to address my goals, concerns, difficulties, etc.	41%	34%	25%	24%	29%	52%
Informal discussions or unscheduled meetings with my P.S. resulting in professional or social discussions	32%	44%	24%	25%	29%	54%
My ED or Sup shows an interest in me and in my problems	26%	43%	31%	24%	16%	40%
Lack of similarity between theory and practice	32%	49%	19%	25%	35%	60%

Table 5.1 Percentage of Other Induction Activities Received

Other Induction Related	Received Less Than Needed	Received What Was Needed	Received More Than Needed	Received Nothing	Received Little	Total None/ Little
Being given a workload which reflects my training and lack of experience	34%	41%	25%	27%	23%	49%
My work is appreciated and commended by my ED or Sup	31%	35%	34%	16%	27%	44%
My ED or Sup promotes a sense of belonging among the educators in our program	31%	38%	31%	21%	26%	47%
Having a procedure available which encourages me to discuss problems caused by my inexperience	39%	25%	36%	26%	29%	55%

who reported receiving none or little, with regard to induction activities. It is important to note that beginning early childhood educators who indicated they received none or little may have also indicated they received what they needed or in fact, received more than what they needed.

Table 5.2 visually demonstrates a summary of what was not received with respect to induction-related activities. Between 43 percent and 52 percent of beginning early childhood educators in this study indicated they received nothing or little in regard to support through such practices as feedback, mentoring, observations, professional development, and other induction activities. Feedback was the area with the highest level of early childhood educators receiving none or little. Again, it is important to note that new educators who indicated they received none or little with respect to support may have also indicated they received what they needed.

Table 5.3 indicates in rank order the top areas where beginning early childhood educators perceived themselves to not get what they needed. The

Table 5.2 Induction Activities: Summary of What Was Not Received

Type of Induction Activity	Average—Received None or Little
Feedback	52% (Column 6; Table 5.1)
Mentoring	51% (Column 6; Table 5.1)
Other	48% (Column 6; Table 5.1)
Observations	45% (Column 6; Table 5.1)
Professional development	43% (Column 6; Table 5.1)
Total average	48% (Column 6; Table 5.1)

Table 5.3 Rank Order of Scales Based on Level of Need

Scale	Range of ECEs Who Reported Receiving Less Than They Needed	Average
Adjustment to New Role	25–53% (Table 2.1; across eight questions)	37%
Adjustment to Field of ECE	19–51% (Table 3.2; across nine questions)	36%
Adjustment to Supervisory Practices	29–41% (Table 4.1; across five questions)	33%
Adjustment to ECE Classroom	19–43% (Table 3.0; across twenty-one questions)	30%
Adjustment to Administrative Practices	19–31% (Table 4.2; across eight questions)	27%
Adjustment to ECE Program	15–30% (Table 2.0; across nine questions)	23%

results are included under each scale section. The highest level of need was found to be under the adjustment to the new role, where between 25 percent and 53 percent of beginning early childhood educators reported receiving less than what they needed.

Summary of Induction Support (from Questionnaire Data)

The highest level of need was found to be under the adjustment to the new role, where between 25 percent and 53 percent of beginning early childhood educators reported receiving less than what they needed. Specific questions related to induction activities such as feedback, observations, professional development, and mentoring were tallied and according to reports from beginning early childhood educators in this study, 49–52 percent receive no or little induction support. While many beginning early childhood educators receive the support they need, 30–50 percent do not.

Findings from Interviews with Beginning Early Childhood Educators

The interview findings reflect the three questions that underpin this study. The first two questions (1) What are beginning early childhood educators' perceptions of their induction experiences in their first year as early childhood educators (2) What, if any, kind(s) of induction support do beginning early childhood educators receive in their first year and how effective are these in supporting beginning early childhood educators' development of professional capacity are answered in Chapters 2 and 4, respectively. The third research question, (3) What, if any, forms of induction or novice professional development would beginning early childhood educators like to take part in, and why, is answered now.

Research Question Three: What, if any, forms of induction or novice Professional development would novice early childhood educators like to take part in, and why?

Early Childhood Educators Want Support for New Educators

All eleven participants reported they would like an induction program that would offer support for novice early childhood educators.

Mentoring

When asked what the ideal induction program would look like, the majority of beginning early childhood educators (6 of 11 [55 percent]) suggested mentoring as one possible strategy. Joel reported:

> The ideal induction program would have the funding to release a staff to be with a new person, even if it was just intermittently throughout the day, just to have a mentor available to you. I'm assuming it would have to come from other staff on your site, but definitely assistance is needed and somebody is required to ask the questions, to observe you, and see the things that you don't notice in your first year, that you might not be doing correctly. It's definitely the form of another person, be it a mentor, or somebody assigned to observe you. That would definitely be the most important in my mind.

Sophie described the characteristics of a mentor: "A strong leader who is passionate about their program and who is supportive and willing to be a mentor too, to be a leader of their program, passionate and also a mentor." Anna described a situation where a beginning educator would act first as an assistant before taking on the full responsibilities as an educator:

> *Just being supportive to them and I'd say that if they were to be an assistant at first—an assistant and then having a lead educator with them, mentoring them, that lead educator to be watching them all the time and noting where they could get help.*

Kim echoed some of Anna's comments regarding easing a new educator into the role:

> *A lot of opportunity to just sit down with them [beginning early childhood educator] and give feedback, let them ask any questions, like what happens in practicum. And giving them the opportunity to not just be pushed in there and hand it all over, "here you go" type of thing, to work with them and show them absolutely everything you can—in a perfect world. Just give them lots of time to get used to it before taking on too much responsibility.*

Elizabeth shared these thoughts on what a mentoring program might look like:

> *I think it would be like a mentoring program. I think to have somebody . . . if you had somebody take that part for three or four hours a week and you could touch base with that person and they could say "What do you want to work on this week?" and if you have any questions, you could ask them then. But I think it's just time—time with an experienced educator.*

Introductions

The majority of the beginning early childhood educators (6 of 11 [55 percent]) want some kind of an introduction to some or all of the following: the children and families; the staff; the program; and the policies, procedures, and philosophy. Alison shared several examples of ways new educators could be introduced to children and families:

> *As far as families go, I would make it mandatory that all of the educators post something about themselves with a picture, like we do in practicum, for families to be introduced to you at the beginning. . . . I also would probably do a family, I mean it would be a little bit impossible to do this every time with a new ECE, but in a perfect world, it would be nice to be able to have a family night with as soon as a new ECE comes in to the room, not for her or anything, but just an organized family night where she has the opportunity with all of the families to introduce herself, talk to them, to get to know them, to see that, you know, see the child with the parents, like all those things I think could benefit them a lot.*

Kathleen shared this about introducing the program to new educators: "*And the orientation for new educators, and sharing the philosophy and sharing the policy they have. That would be really helpful.*" Having introductions to children, families, staff, and the program can be beneficial for new educators as it can provide them with the opportunity to learn about the community they are now a part of.

Professional Development

Many beginning early childhood educators (5 of 11 [45 percent]) suggested professional development be part of the induction program. Kim suggested it was important for novice early childhood educators to take part in professional development: "*Any workshops that come available—go to them. Any extra education that you can get helps, because it's always changing too.*" Connie talked about professional development being available to the entire staff:

> *I think that professional development should happen as . . . the employees of a program as a whole, I think that we should have opportunities to, for example, either the whole staff goes somewhere to attend something or someone is brought in to work with the staff.*

Supportive Work Environment

Some (5 of 11 [45 percent]) of the beginning early childhood educators reported that a supportive work environment should be part of an ideal induction program.

When asked about the ideal induction program, new early childhood educators shared the following aspects of a supportive work environment: novice educators are valued, leaders who provoke thinking in novice educators and experienced educators, extra staff, clear communication and delineation on responsibilities, information on professional development, clear communication, and professional development for experienced educators. Emma talked about the importance of novice early childhood educators being valued in the work environment:

> *We can't really see them [beginning early childhood educator] as an incompetent somebody, who doesn't really know. We can't really see them as empty vase. . . . They are not empty vase. They have something there already. . . . Try to bring that out. Help them to bring that out. But also collaborative means both sides, right? New people, experienced people also learn something new. So we work together. That is the collaboration that I am talking about. And it is lacking. I think it is lacking. . . . My ideal situation is, there is a supervisor in the centre and her job is to create the environment where colleagues, I mean people, like educators can work together.*

Sarah wondered about offering professional development to experienced educators to support them in their knowledge of what beginning early childhood educators need:

> I mean do you offer a workshop to all managers, to all directors, to all senior educators, whatever you want to call them. And say, if you get a new ECE, who's been in the field for less than five years, these are some warning signs you want to watch for. These are some things you want to be aware of. To educate those who are in that position how to receive a first year, on how to support novice ECEs.

Sarah went further in discussing the possibility that the people in the workplace take some responsibility for inducting the new educator:

> Because maybe it's not me as an educator. Maybe it was the job site receiving and early childhood educator, that's what I'm saying, don't put it all on the new ECE to say, "Oh well, I'm It's so hard for them to be a new ECE". Put it on them that they get these new people and they don't even know how to train them because they've had staff that just knows what to do.

Support from the Early Childhood Education Community

A few (3 of 11 [27 percent]) of the novice early childhood educators indicated support from the early childhood education community would be important in an ideal induction program.

When asked about the ideal induction program, new early childhood educators shared several ideas related to support from the early childhood education community: social gatherings for beginning early childhood educators, opportunities to visit and observe other childcare centers, induction standards, and an early childhood educators' network. In talking about the support she received through social gatherings with peers, Sarah wondered about how this might extend to support novice educators:

> I'm also the type that if during that beer night/pub night one of my classmates says, "Oh my God, at my job site right now this is going on", I'm the first that would say to them, "Have you considered looking elsewhere for work?" Because I would know that it might be helpful knowing where they've come from, going maybe what I'm hearing them gripe about that kind of support is necessary for all kinds of new educators.

Connie talked of the importance of observing different centers prior to choosing one to work in:

> *I think that observation of the program would be the very first step. That's something that I think is really important. After a few years I've come to realize that having a chance to actually maybe observe and participate a little bit in several different programs before choosing one to work in.*

Connie discussed the idea of having standards in place for induction activities:

> *I think if things aren't standardized, then it cannot happen easily. Maybe it starts out as being really structured and organized and whatever, but then they maybe open another centre and then it starts to be busier and then some things . . . you know, now we have less staff meetings just because everyone is too busy, and I think it's really easy for those important things to fall to the side because it's not like an immediate . . . I don't know, I think when things start to get really busy like that, for example having multiple programs all under the same thing or whatever, you start to kind of triage your time, you decide what's the most important thing that I need to deal with right now, and I think that the needs of the employees are kind of last on the list. I don't know . . . . I think in our field, because you have the children you are dealing with which is the number one, and then you have the parents, and then you have all the stuff that goes with those two things, and I think that the needs of the staff can easily fall to the side, when you have lots of those other things that are kind of pending.*

This chapter included findings related to induction support received by novice early childhood educators. Specific questions related to induction activities such as feedback, observations, professional development, and mentoring were tallied and according to reports from beginning early childhood educators in this study, 49–52 percent receive no or little induction support, the average being 49 percent. While many beginning early childhood educators receive the support they need, 30–50 percent do not. Through a coding process, several themes emerged from the qualitative data, and this was shared throughout the previous chapters. These included specific information on the kinds of experiences first-year early childhood educators have, what types of support they receive, whether or not they participate in induction activities, and what forms of induction they would like to see in place for future educators. In Chapter 6, I will discuss the key themes from the previous chapters while also showing alignment between the research shared and previous works.

6

Key Themes

The Work Is Both Overwhelming and Deeply Satisfying

In seeking to answer the first research question, what are beginning early childhood educators' perceptions of their induction experiences in their first year as early childhood educators, the main theme that has emerged from the analysis of the data is that beginning early childhood educators find the work to be both overwhelming and deeply satisfying. This finding is similar to the results from other studies where early childhood educators found the nature of the work itself to be both their greatest source of satisfaction and frustration (Jorde-Bloom, 1988; Kwon et al., 2020). A description of the overwhelming nature of the work will occur first, followed by a discussion on the work as being deeply satisfying. In describing the stages of educator development, Katz (1972) portrayed an early childhood educator's first year as being one of survival, where one tries to get through the day. This theory fits well with this study's finding, which supports the idea that beginning early childhood educators feel overwhelmed with the work in their first year. Moreover, part of the overwhelming nature of the work comes from the reality that beginning early childhood educators are given the same workload as experienced educators (Kearney, 2011). For example, in this study, 34 percent of beginning early childhood educators reported they did not get the support needed with regard to a workload that reflected their training and lack of experience. Further to this, 49 percent of the participants reported receiving no or little support in this area. This aligns well with work done by (Feiman-Nemser et al.,1999) who wrote that beginning teachers are often given the most challenging of workloads. In addition, the OECD (n.d.) has recognized the importance of workload and the impact it has on educator retention as well as the ability to meet the needs of children and families. Furthermore, in some cases, the busyness of the first weeks on the job results in a failure to ensure necessary information is communicated, leaving educators to figure things out on their own (Chubbuck et al., 2001). In reviewing the data analysis, the following subjects arose as areas where new educators need particular support. These are: dealing with philosophical differences among educators, knowing how to handle guidance of children's behavior, and knowing how to organize one's time for programming planning. With regard to philosophical differences among educators, for some their experience in the workplace is one where there is little time to deal with issues such as the philosophy of the program. In this study, 22 percent of beginning early childhood educators reported receiving less than what they needed regarding understanding the philosophy of the program. Further to this, 34 percent reported receiving no support in understanding the philosophy of the program. Sarah described her experiences as being one of "sink or swim" and where the program philosophy was very different than what she was used to. The idea of being left on one's own to "figure it out" concurs with a study by Nicholson and Reifel (2011), where educators described their experiences in the same way. This is critical because beginning early childhood educators need the support from colleagues as they make the transition from student educators to fully qualified early childhood educators (Aitken & Harford, 2010). Furthermore, Ingersoll (2012) found that having time to plan and work with other teachers was the strongest factor in reducing teacher attrition.

Despite the overwhelming workload reported by beginning early childhood educators in this study, a large majority (89 percent) of participants reported high levels of satisfaction from their work as an early childhood educator. The finding of high job satisfaction resonates well with studies in Australia and the UK conducted by McDonald, Thorpe, & Irvine (2018), and Cameron, Josephson, & Chua (2001), who found that educators of young children were satisfied with the work because of their love and commitment to working with children. Likewise, beginning early childhood educators in the current study also spoke about the joy of being part of children's development. Additionally, 68 percent of these new early childhood educators in British Columbia agreed or strongly agreed that they would choose to go into the field of early childhood education again. Similarly, Ozgun (2005) found that nearly 88 percent of Turkish early childhood educators were very satisfied with their work. While in the same study, 78.5 percent of Turkish early childhood educators said they would choose the profession again if they had the choice. Jorde-Bloom (1988) found that 83 percent of early childhood educators in the United States would choose the career again. However, a study in 2021 found "Only 34% of ECE staff [in the United States] reported being very satisfied with their work compared to 49% of the national workforce" (Farewell et al., 2022). Thus, as with some past studies in other countries, educators find the work to be highly satisfying. These results are in spite of challenges faced by early childhood educators such as low wage, overwhelming workload, high expectations to perform, and a lack of societal respect. As there are connections between job satisfaction and teacher efficacy, the high job satisfaction may mean that early childhood educators in this study have higher levels of teacher efficacy. At the least, such high job satisfaction among beginning early childhood educators in British Columbia is especially interesting when one considers that half of all early childhood educators in British Columbia leave the field in the first five years of work (Early Childhood Educators of British Columbia, 2012; CBC News, 2022).

Summary

Beginning early childhood educators in British Columbia find the workload to be overwhelming while being deeply satisfied with their work with children. This finding is similar to other studies with both beginning early childhood educators and teachers.

The Induction Support Beginning Early Childhood Educators in British Columbia Receive Is Haphazard

In analyzing the findings related to the second research question, What, if any, kind(s) of induction support do beginning early childhood educators receive in their first year and how effective are these in supporting beginning early childhood educators' development of professional capacity, what became clear is that the induction support that beginning early childhood educators in British Columbia receive is haphazard, meaning that the support received is inconsistent. In other words, based on the findings from this study, beginning early childhood educators in British Columbia cannot assume they will receive the induction support needed in their first year. Results showed it was very much dependent on the particular job site, the educators on site, and the level of turnover among staff. As was pointed out in the introduction, there are no formal structures in place to support beginning early childhood educators in British Columbia. The fact that beginning early childhood educators have specific induction needs has been well documented, and Chubbuck et al. (2001) found that novice teachers wanted both information and supportive relationships with other educators. Induction can refer to both the time period when a new educator is being introduced to the field of early childhood education as well as the specific induction activities that may take place, including mentoring, professional development, feedback on practice, and observations (Aitken et al., 2008). It is important to note that induction is not a perfect solution and, in some cases, induction activities prove unhelpful. Research studies on induction programs have found that the context is important; thus a "one-size-fits-all" approach should be avoided (Fresko & Nasser-Abu Alhija, 2008). The provincial association representing early childhood educators, ECEBC, has been actively involved in looking at ways to understand and address some of the issues facing new early childhood educators. Winstead Fry (2010) conducted a case study of an unsuccessful new teachers' induction experience, finding that the beginning teacher thought the induction meetings were repetitious, and contrary to what Ingersoll (2012) has reported as being important, she did not have common planning time or a regular time to meet with her mentor. Further to this she did not feel that she had a good rapport with her mentor.

Gay (2007), a researcher working with ECEBC, suggested a mentoring program be put in place. This has certainly been something that other countries have provided. In New Zealand, early childhood educators take part in much longer training time which includes being provisionally registered prior to attaining fully qualified and certified status. Embedded in this particular model is a range of support that includes assigned mentors, observations, feedback, and professional development (Aitken et al., 2008). One must be careful, however, to assume that mentoring would work successfully for everyone. Fantili and McDougall (2009) found that simply assigning mentors to protégées was not the answer. Participants had mentors who were not qualified, which led to frustrating experiences for the new teachers. Additionally, some participants did not connect relationally with the mentor, making it difficult to form the necessary bond. Participants identified various issues related to how mentoring might work and Emma, in particular, talked about the importance of experienced educators being current.

I want to try documentation, pedagogical narrations, but some people really strongly disagree with that practice and then I feel like my learning is actually stopped there. I studied something new and I believe that it is important to this field, but then I try to bring that into the field and I am stopped. Like because they have more seniority and they are more experienced, they kind of see me as incompetent and sometimes I feel like I am told, "Hey what are you talking about? That's nonsense. Period. Stop". I feel like there's no faith that I can be. I have to stop myself there. And that's a huge dilemma. Then I just say to myself, "Why am I spending so much time and money and study and can't even use the knowledge?"

In this particular quotation, we have a beginning early childhood educator who is doing innovative work, but who does not have the support of her immediate superior. Should this person be her mentor? It seems simplistic to think that simply identifying someone with experience makes that person a good role model. Again, when asked what makes the difference between a good, experienced educator versus an early childhood educator who is experienced, but not helpful, one participant acknowledged the importance of staying current. In other words, the support one receives is very much dependent on the particular jobsite one is working in and the educators one is working alongside. When looking at this example through the theoretical lens of the theory of adult learning, it is important that this beginning early childhood educator received the assistance and support she both needed and for which she was ready. Furthermore, without the support required, her level of teacher efficacy may be lowered, impacting her ability to develop her identity as a professional and her ability to remain in the profession. In a study by Long (2004), new teachers wanted administrative and collegial support. New teachers expected enthusiasm for new ideas from their colleagues, but instead experienced colleagues who seemed disinterested in moving forward, which is the same as some of the participants of this study. New teachers were infuriated with the lack of passion demonstrated by their assigned mentors. Some of the interview participants spoke about the dramatically different levels of support they received from one job to another and this is consistent with a study by Fresko and Nasser-Abu Alhija (2008) who found that finding a mentor within a school setting was challenging. Moreover, the level of support received from the mentors proved to be unpredictable, with some new teachers receiving a lot of support and others receiving very little. It is also important to recognize that the beginning early childhood educators in this study want to feel appreciated and valued. Anna realized she still needed support, but wanted the communication to be constructive and less critical: "*We don't know all the things that a ten-year ECE knows. . . . It would be nice if they could remind me of things or have constructive criticism instead of it just being criticism.*" As revealed in the current study and as Knowles (2012) asserted, beginning early childhood educators bring prior experiences that should be valued. Indeed, a new educator in the current study suggested that prior experience should be "drawn out" and supported.

Summary

The induction support that beginning early childhood educators receive in British Columbia is haphazard, meaning it is inconsistent, and not something educators can assume they will receive. Previous research on the induction of both teachers and early childhood educators has found similar findings and although not emulated in the current study, the results include a high turnover of staff, as educators leave the profession prior to completing an induction process and/or educators who have left the liberation of their training experiences in favor of a more conservative programming philosophy.

Beginning Early Childhood Educators in British Columbia Would Like Induction Support in the Form of Mentoring or Peer Support, Observations, Feedback, and Professional Development

In identifying the key theme for research question three, what, if any, forms of induction or novice professional development would beginning early childhood educators like to take part in, and why, I determined that beginning early childhood educators in British Columbia would like induction support in the forms of mentoring or peer support, observations, feedback, and professional development. New early childhood educators who identified themselves as having taken part in some or all of the above induction activities spoke highly of the experiences, voicing the importance of these kinds of experiences in their initial year as an early childhood educator. Similarly, mentoring is one of the induction activities which has been described as a strategy to define professional standards and can help to influence the profession over time (Devos, 2010; Poulter Jewson, 2020). Moreover, in addition to producing changes to one's practice, mentoring may lead to beginning teachers finding new ways of understanding themselves and their identity as teachers. The idea that new early childhood educators in this study would like to receive induction fits well with a report from the OECD (2005) where it was suggested that the education of teaching be viewed as a continuum, not simply what one does while in a post-secondary setting. In other words, despite the fact that beginning early childhood educators in British Columbia have graduated and have received their certification from the province, they still require support and help as they transition into the role of an early childhood educator. Sadly, beginning early childhood educators in this study reported that this kind of support and help is not widely available and for some beginning educators, their employers seem to be satisfied with the minimum licensing requirement—that the employees have a license from the province. This finding fits well with previous research with new teachers who indicated they needed social networks in which to find support for their new roles (Sabar, 2004). The lack of induction support in the form of feedback, observations on practice, mentoring, and professional development is an issue identified by Cameron,

Mooney, Owen, and Moss (2001) who reported 14 percent of educators left the field due to a lack of feedback and staff supervision from management. In a study by Rolfe (2005), it was reported that many workplaces were ill-equipped to be inducting beginning early childhood educators. For example, in Rolfe's study, educators were provided with very little introduction to the childcare program. Additionally, as in this study of beginning early childhood educators in British Columbia, educators typically took on full duties on the first day of employment, rather than having a workload that recognized their status as a beginning educator.

Beginning early childhood educators in British Columbia are not receiving the support they need to understand the services of ECEBC and/or to become members in either the local and/or provincial branch, leaving a potential gap for educators to be supported in this area. Interestingly, in some cases, educators indicated they received more support than they felt they needed within their first year. What is the communication like between new and experienced early childhood educators? Are there open discussions about what one needs support with? Furthermore, what kind of communication occurs between administrators and their staff? Are experienced educators engaged in a conversation about how to support new educators? One new educator who received mentoring, albeit for a short period of time as the mentor left the job, indicated the mentor was not assigned; rather she was simply someone he felt comfortable with. Others worked with experienced staff but did not feel a sense of mentorship. Based on this, I believe that the level of support for new educators is very "hit and miss," meaning they may or may not receive the support needed and very much dependent on the job site and the particular educators there. In a study by Nicholson and Reifel (2011), a beginning early childhood educator spoke of a similar reality, saying that nothing was clearly communicated to the experienced educator about mentoring the new educator. Instead, they were simply introduced to each other and left to get to work. Unfortunately, this is similar to Sarah who was told, "*Here's the room, here's the kids, take care of them.*"

Beginning early childhood educators in this study are not receiving the induction support they want and need, and this is due to several factors, including a lack of supervisory visits to the classroom, little or no time to discuss programming and/or individual concerns, a lack of support to help them cope with feelings of frustration and/or inadequacy. Furthermore, beginning early childhood educators in the current study needed additional support in knowing how to deal with the low respect given to those working with very young children. This echoed the results from a study by Cameron et al. (2001) who reported a low valuing of educators working with young children, leading some to leave the field. Moreover, a study of the professional identity of early childhood educators in Ireland reported educators thought they were perceived to be "just the babysitter" (Moloney, 2010, p. 177). New early childhood educators in this study indicated they wanted support from experienced educators. This may include coworkers, supervisors, or executive directors. Many beginning early childhood educators in British Columbia form connections with and receive support from a colleague at work. This is consistent with other studies, such as one by Nicholson and Reifel (2011) where the participants indicated they learned the most about how to be an early childhood educator from their colleagues at work. In another study, novice teachers reported they wanted a network of support where they could share problems and ideas without the worry of being evaluated (Chubbuck et al., 2001). In the study proper, new educators did not get the support they needed with regard to the lack of similarity between theory and practice and this concurs with Flores and Day (2006) who found there were tensions between what was learned at university and the reality of the classroom. These findings point to the importance of beginning early childhood educators receiving support on the jobsite. Furthermore, when new teachers find they are lacking the necessary knowledge and are not getting the support they need, this can result in a crisis of identity. This crisis of identity can further impact the teacher efficacy of beginning early childhood educators. Bandura (1997) asserted the idea that how one thinks about one's ability to make changes and in fact be a producer, not simply a product of the environment, impacts one's efficacy. Beginning early childhood educators need adequate support in order to grow in their teacher efficacy, their belief in their own abilities as an educator. The workplace seems to be well set up for this kind of support, but as the results from this study indicate, not all early childhood education workplaces offer support to new early childhood educators. What kinds of barriers might stand in the way of induction support through the workplace? Luft, Roehig, and Patterson (2002) identified the following barriers to an induction program for secondary science teachers: identifying key administrators, recruiting participants, inconsistent ideologies, university support, and time constraints. The findings from this study indicate that beginning early childhood educators in British Columbia need and want to take part in induction-related activities which will help them as they transition into their professional identities, and currently the College of Early Childhood Educators of Ontario is considering the implementation of an induction program (Government of Ontario, 2013).

Summary

Beginning early childhood educators in British Columbia would like to have access to induction support in the form of mentoring or peer support, observations, feedback, and professional development. Recent literature on induction programs was presented, which helped to provide a rationale for the need of induction, while pointing out the danger in thinking induction support is a panacea for all of the problems facing beginning early childhood educators.

Practical and Theoretical Implications

From the three major findings, a major implication that addresses all research questions is that the early childhood education workplace is ideally suited for new educators to be successfully inducted into the profession and to form their professional identity (Flores & Day, 2006). This idea fits very well with the "communities of practice" theory put forth by Lave and Wenger (1998), where learning is viewed as something that occurs through participation, not solely in the mind of an individual. Moreover, in communities of practice, individuals come together to "figure out how our engagement fits in the broader scheme of things" (Wenger, 1998, p. 162). Despite the fact that it was not consistent for all beginning early childhood educators, 41 percent of beginning early childhood educators in this study reported receiving great or very great support with regard to forming a connection with an experienced educator; 35 percent of beginning early childhood educators reported receiving great or very great support in feeling comfortable interacting with all staff; and 29 percent of beginning early childhood educators reported they received great or very great opportunities to observe early childhood educators. Beginning early childhood educators in this study reported they receive support from colleagues. In spite of the lack of uniform support, there is a baseline on which to build. Beginning educators working alongside experienced educators can gain perspective on who they are and what their identity is as an early childhood educator. This kind of support model is similar to the one used in Worcestershire, England (Murray, 2006), where critical peers are used instead of mentors. In this model, the emphasis is not on being an experienced educator, but instead, being someone who will support and provoke, asking the tough questions. Furthermore, this idea fits well with the theory of adult learning where Knowles advocated for learning situations to be problem based and offered as a choice to adults.

This idea of using the workplace as the learning environment for new educators aligns well with the theory of adult learning, which places importance on the experiences of the learner (Knowles, Holton, & Swanson, 2012). In this kind of model, the educators, the novice, and the more experienced educator can benefit. Though a theory based on children's learning, Vygotsky's theory of zones of proximal development seems to fit well within the context of workplace support and/or learning. Perhaps it is because educators are being supported in their moment of need—in that place of what they know and what they need to know. This concept of readiness to learn, from the theory of adult learning, is critical for those involved in teaching and/or supporting new early childhood educators. When do we teach the information that is needed? When is the learner deeded ready to learn? Knowles, Holton, and Swanson (2012) asserted that adults "become ready to learn when their life situation creates a need to know" (p. 192). They went on to suggest that the more "adult learning professionals can anticipate and understand adults' life situations and readiness for learning, the more effective they can be" (pp. 192–3). Here it would seem that the team-centered approach that is common in most early childhood settings is poised to support new educators as they learn through their zone of proximal development when they are ready to learn. Wenger and Lave (1991) wrote this about identities: "We conceive of identities as long-term, living relations between persons and their place and participation in communities of practice. Thus identity, knowing, and social membership entail one another" (p. 53). The findings from this study indicate that a significant number of beginning early childhood educators (30–50 percent) are in workplaces that do not operate under the idea of communities of practice. These are workplaces where beginning early childhood educators are left on their own to figure things out, instead of having the potential benefit of learning alongside experienced educators, for the purposes of forming a professional identity. This type of environment is in contrast to the ideas put forth by Sachs (2000) who reported that networks based on mutual trust can develop into ongoing learning communities where learning occurs for everyone involved. Additionally, over half of beginning early childhood educators in British Columbia reported they do not receive the help necessary to learn about the services offered by the provincial organization representing their interests. Furthermore, the professional association is a place where new early childhood educators can go to for support. For example, there are local branches across the province. Additionally, professional development is offered regularly. These are important things for all educators to be aware of and in particular, new educators. The fact that new educators in this study were not aware of the services of the professional organization is particularly concerning when one looks at Wenger's idea that identity is formed through community membership that entails: "mutual engagement, a joint enterprise, and a shared repertoire" (1998, p. 152). Additionally, Sachs (2000) asserted that networks are a way to "direct the agenda of teacher professionalism" (p. 88).

In this chapter the key findings from the qualitative and quantitative data were presented. They are as follows: the work is both overwhelming and deeply satisfying; the induction support beginning early childhood educators in British Columbia receive is haphazard; and beginning early childhood educators in British Columbia would like induction support in the form of mentoring or peer support, observations, feedback, and professional development. As demonstrated, this study's conclusions concur with theories and previous studies and provide additional "nuanced" understandings. In the next section of the book, Part II, implications and recommendations will be shared through the lens of best practice for early childhood educators. Additionally, theories and new directions for early childhood education will be discussed, with an aim to show what is possible.

Part II

Moving Forward

7

Toward a Best Practice for Early Childhood Educators

The Work Is Both Overwhelming and Deeply Satisfying

The first major finding from this research study is that beginning early childhood educators in British Columbia perceive the work to be both overwhelming and deeply satisfying. Although at first glance this appears to be a contradiction, this finding resonated with other research studies on the experiences of beginning early childhood educators, as was discussed in the preceding chapter. Novice early childhood educators in British Columbia find themselves working in a high-paced environment where the expectations placed on them are the same as those with considerable experience. Because the workplace environment is one where there is a high turnover of staff, beginning early childhood educators often find themselves stepping into leadership roles quickly, and in some cases, within the first six months on the job. Compounding this issue is the reality that beginning early childhood educators may be working with other new educators and/or have supervisors who are new to their leadership roles, meaning that needed support may not be received due to the fact that everyone is in their own form of "survival" as depicted by Katz (1972). Despite the challenging work conditions, a high majority of beginning early childhood educators in this study reported deep satisfaction with the work. Further to this, most said they would choose the field of early childhood education again if given the chance, which means that the profession has attracted dedicated people who are committed to the profession.

The Induction Support Beginning Early Childhood Educators Receive in British Columbia Is Haphazard

The second major finding from this inquiry is that though early childhood educators in British Columbia receive induction support through such practices as mentoring or peer support, observations, feedback, and professional development, it is haphazard at best, with few receiving adequate assistance. Beginning early childhood educators who do not receive adequate induction support often feel isolated and alone, a finding discussed in previous studies.

Beginning Early Childhood Educators in British Columbia Would Like Induction Support in the Form of Mentoring or Peer Support, Observations, Feedback, and Professional Development

The third major finding from this research study is that beginning early childhood educators in British Columbia would like to take part in induction-related activities. All beginning early childhood educators in this study who took part in the semi-structured interviews reported they wanted to be involved in induction activities. When given the opportunity to express other needs related to their adjustment to the field of early childhood education, beginning early childhood educators who took part in the online questionnaire expressed a wide range of thoughts regarding their need for support. This included the need for support to be given to new educators through such aspects as having time to plan and discuss programming and/or differences in philosophy, to receive constructive feedback rather than criticism, and to be given opportunities for professional development.

Introduction of New Knowledge

Models of Perception

Many beginning early childhood educators in British Columbia cannot assume they will receive the induction support they need as they enter the field of early childhood education. New early childhood educators who do not receive adequate support believe they are perceived in one or more of the following ways: as an empty vessel, knowing nothing; as someone who is licensed or certified and ready to go; as one who needs to learn how things are done in the real world; and as one who needs nothing. Figure 7.0 depicts the perceptions early childhood educators have regarding how they are viewed in their workplaces.

Figure 7.0 Model of how new educators are perceived. © Laura K. Doan.

Licensed and Ready to Go

Some beginning early childhood educators in British Columbia are left on their own, without adequate induction support during their first year of work. It is as if they are viewed as fully prepared, or "licensed [or certified] and ready to go," when in fact novice early childhood educators in this study reported they did not want to be left on their own.

Needs Nothing

The concept of being "licensed and ready to go" is linked to the idea that the beginning early childhood educator needs nothing. It may come from a view that early childhood educators have already received what they need through their post-secondary training and now need to get on with the work of performing as an educator. Some beginning early childhood educators in this study reported being left alone to figure things out on their own.

Needs to Learn How Things Are Done in the "Real World"

Some early childhood educators in British Columbia feel undervalued by their coworkers. Attempts to bring new programming ideas into the classroom that had been learned in the educator's recent education were re-buffed, and due to an environment where those with seniority held the power, the new educator felt "shut down." This ties in well with the idea that the new early childhood educator needs to learn how things are done in the real world. The transition from student to fully fledged early childhood educator is a difficult one for some educators as they encounter workplaces with little support by way of feedback, observations, professional development, and mentoring or peer support. This is in contrast to what early childhood education students typically receive at a post-secondary institute: regular feedback on their practice, observations done on themselves as well as the opportunity to observe others, opportunities for professional development, and time to work with experienced educators.

Empty Vessel: Knows Nothing

This is very much related to the preceding idea, and it is a way of looking at beginning educators as not having anything to add. It is the antithesis of viewing the early childhood educator as being a team player, ready to help and add to the workplace environment. Despite their novice status, beginning early childhood educators are not empty vessels, ready to be filled. Rather, they are ready and willing to contribute to the learning environment.

Figure 7.1 portrays how beginning early childhood educators would like to be viewed and subsequently treated in their places of work.

Value Me

Beginning early childhood educators who took part in this study reported they want to be valued by their coworkers and supervisors. Educators who felt valued, described situations where experienced educators collaborated with them by sharing programming ideas and by asking for their thoughts and ideas. In other words, even though beginning educators lacked experience, they were recognized as having something to offer. Despite their desire for induction support, new early childhood educators want to know they are valued for the work they do and the skills they have to offer. One new educator spoke about the need to be recognized as having value, and not being perceived as "an empty vase." In other words, beginning early childhood educators have something to offer despite their novice status, and that contribution should be valued.

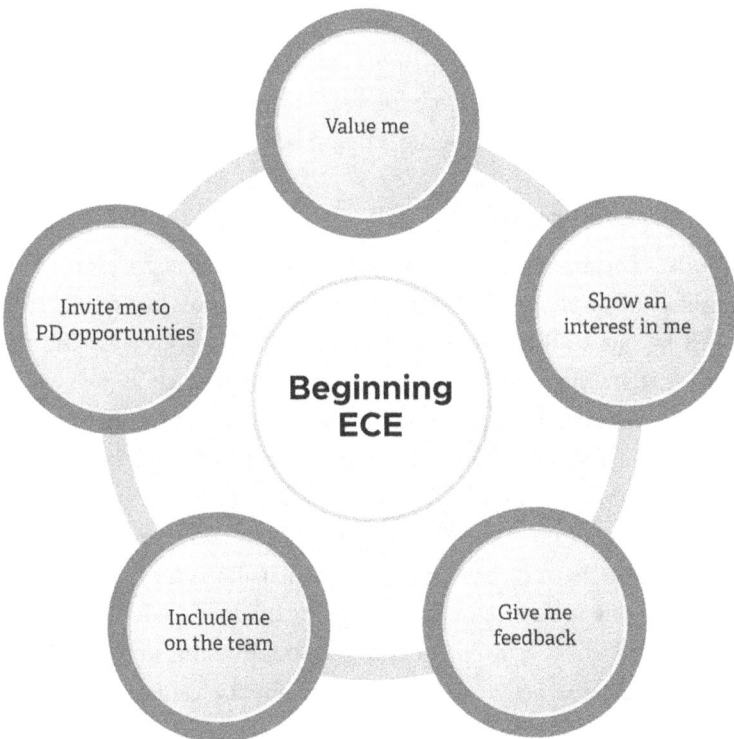

Figure 7.1 How beginning early childhood educators want to be treated. © Laura K. Doan.

Show an Interest in Me

Furthermore, beginning early childhood educators want coworkers and supervisors to take an interest in them. This may include intentional communication with the beginning early childhood educator regarding how their induction is going. Whatever form it takes, this requires someone in the workplace who cares and takes the time to show the beginning educator that they are interested in their welfare.

Give Me Feedback

Beginning early childhood educators want feedback. As mentioned previously, performance feedback is a regular occurrence for early childhood education students, and educators in this study wanted feedback in the form of reviews of their practice as it was seen as something to help them in knowing how they were doing in their new role. This could take several forms including informal verbal feedback throughout the day and formal employee evaluations. Beginning early childhood educators who receive informal and/or formal feedback find it helpful to them as they may not know if their perceptions of their own performance are accurate. In contrast, new early childhood educators who do not receive any feedback feel alone and abandoned at a time when they need the feedback most.

Include Me on the Team

The majority of beginning early childhood educators in British Columbia are not working alone in an educational setting. For example, most beginning educators are joined by one to three other colleagues in their workplaces. The concept of "team" is something that is taught and put into practice in post-secondary early childhood education preparation programs, but what happens in the workplace can be very different. Some beginning early childhood educators do not experience a feeling of being part of a team. In some cases, beginning early childhood educators find themselves in work environments where there is a definite hierarchy and chain of command that allows for little in the way of innovation or new ideas from beginning early childhood educators. This is in direct contrast to what beginning early childhood educators in British Columbia want, which is to be an active, contributing member of teams in the workplace.

Invite Me to Professional Development Opportunities

Beginning early childhood educators in this study want more opportunities for professional development and they want to hear about them from the jobsite they work in. This includes paid time off to attend professional development as well as monetary support to cover the cost of professional development opportunities, which usually are the responsibility of the early childhood educator. Beginning early childhood educators are in a place in their career where they need to have opportunities to gain information that affects their practice. Additionally, beginning early childhood educators need professional development for the purposes of meeting other educators in the community, as some early childhood education workplaces have few people on staff.

What Needs to Happen in Order to Bring This Change About?

In order for beginning early childhood educators to receive the support they want and need, I recommend that the jobsite be viewed as a community of practice, not simply as a job. Some employers and some early childhood educators see the early childhood education workplace as simply a job, not a community of practice, and that is very different. When the early childhood education workplace is viewed as a job, beginning early childhood educators are not adequately supported and inducted into the profession.

Prior to working, early childhood education students receive a wide range of support from various partners associated with the post-secondary institution where they are receiving training. Early childhood education students receive support from their peers in the classroom (fellow early childhood education students), early childhood education instructors, sponsor educators, and the greater early childhood education community. A sense of community can be developed within the post-secondary classroom. Also, instructors attempt to engage students into the greater community of early childhood education by bringing in various guest speakers representing diverse childcare programs and ECEBC, the provincial organization representing early childhood educators in British Columbia. Within the context of the post-secondary early childhood education setting, students are involved in regular, daily communication with instructors, program administrators, sponsor educators, community members, and fellow students that is face-to-face, online, and/or via telephone.

Figure 7.2 The isolated ECE workplace. © Laura K. Doan.

Once early childhood education students graduate and leave the post-secondary setting, entering the workforce, there may be little to no induction support. Figure 7.2 demonstrates the isolation that many beginning early childhood educators experience within their jobs.

This isolated workplace represents little to no induction support, where beginning early childhood educators are simply shown the room of children and told to begin working. The large circle represents the workplace community that all parties are involved in. The smaller circles represent that individuals are separate and have no lines of connection, as they work independently of each other.

In order for beginning early childhood educators to receive the induction support they need, the jobsite needs to be viewed as a community of practice. This will be discussed in detail further on, after a portrayal of how the conclusions from this research result in additions to theory on educator development.

Additions to Theory

In addition to helping to bring about practical change to the field of early childhood education, this study has the possibility of adding to the theory on educator development. This study of beginning early childhood educators relied heavily on the work of Katz (1972) who put forth a developmental model for educator development that included the following four stages: survival, consolidation, renewal, and maturity. While discussing the needs of the beginning early childhood educator in the survival stage, Katz identified the need for instruction from people on the jobsite such as "senior staff members, advisors, consultants or program assistants" (p. 4). Considering that Katz's work was completed in the early seventies, it is disappointing that beginning early childhood educators continue to find themselves working in environments not suitable for their developmental needs. The results from this study agree with the model from Katz in the sense that beginning early childhood educators are experiencing a sense of survival, often finding themselves in workplaces where they feel overwhelmed, isolated, and alone. While Katz's model has a lot to offer by way of understanding educator development, it implies that change happens within the individual, but the findings from this study suggest otherwise. The results from this study indicate the growth that happens for beginning early childhood educators takes place within a community of practice, within both the workplace and in the greater early childhood education community, as outlined by Lave and Wenger (1991).

While Katz discussed various strategies of support that beginning early childhood educators need, the focus remained on the individuals, not on the workplace community. Early childhood education workplaces need to be viewed as communities of practice, where beginning early childhood educators can be successfully inducted into the profession through such activities as mentoring or peer support, receiving feedback, having the opportunity for mutual observations, and professional development. Furthermore, while the model put forward by Katz suggested that the supporting educators need to be people in authority, the results from this study indicate the support can come from coworkers. More important than one's title or role is the level of support beginning early childhood educators want to receive from another educator. Furthermore, the results from this study indicate the importance of having experienced educators who are current, that is, educators who are both open to and aware of new ways of programming for children's optimal learning and development.

The model put forth by Katz focused on the needs of beginning early childhood educators in the survival year. There seems to be no mention of those attributes that beginning early childhood educators contribute to the teaching setting in their first year. That is where the results from this study are different, indicating that indeed, beginning early childhood educators have much to offer the workplace environment, despite their novice status. Beginning early childhood educators in this study indicated they want to be valued and to be part of the team. Beginning early childhood educators are ready to contribute to the learning environment by bringing in new programming ideas, despite the fact that it may be their first year of teaching. Thus, the results from this study indicate that many beginning early childhood educators have a different trajectory from the model put forth by Katz. Each person can be involved in supporting beginning early childhood educators and much can be done to build a culture of practice where this occurs.

Recommendations

Doan Model of Best Practice for the Induction of Beginning Early Childhood Educators

The Doan model of best practice for the induction of beginning early childhood educators is based on the positive findings from this research, that beginning early childhood educators who do receive support, do so from their workplace and/or the greater early childhood education community (Figure 7.3). It is future oriented

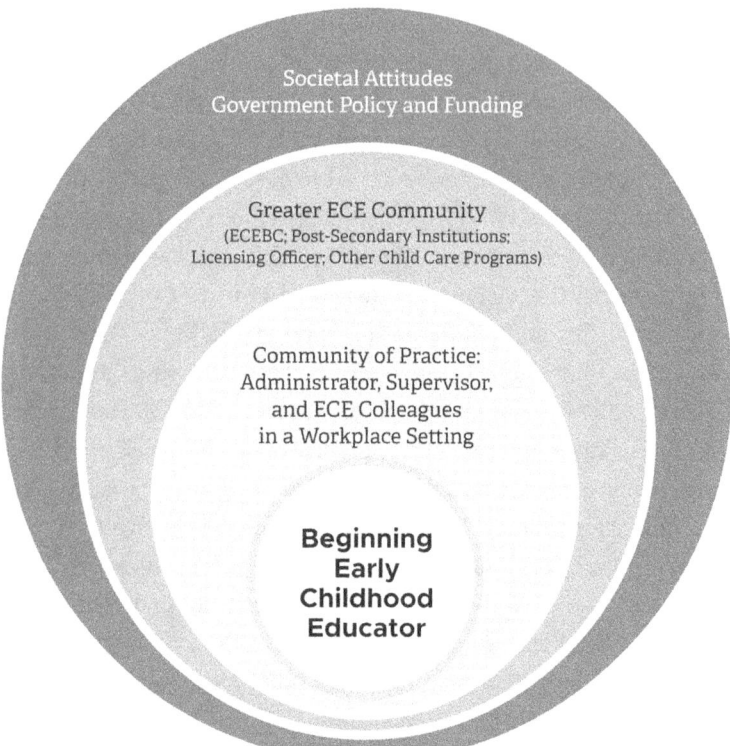

Figure 7.3 The Doan model of best practice for the induction of beginning early childhood educators. © Laura K. Doan.

and implies change is needed in order to move to a system where all beginning educators are supported. In this model, beginning early childhood educators are positioned in the first circle, representing their importance and the significance of the support they should receive. Beginning early childhood educators who participated in this study indicated the work was both overwhelming and deeply satisfying. Furthermore, participants wanted a program of support for beginning early childhood educators. The participants who did receive induction support did so in the workplace from fellow educators, supervisors, or administrators. Additionally, participants received support from the greater early childhood education community, such as post-secondary faculty, licensing officers, and educators from other childcare centers. Therefore, in this model which is described using future tense, the beginning early childhood educator is surrounded by a community of practice that includes supportive colleagues who are able to engage in mentoring and/or peer support. Support is context-specific, not "cookie cutter." Every early childhood center is unique; staff groups have different strengths and challenges, and new early childhood educators have different needs and abilities. Therefore, this is not a "one-size-fits-all" approach. The induction support is consistently offered, but it is based on the context of the specific community of practice and the individual needs of the beginning early childhood educator. Given the new addition of theory, this model is not based on the underlying assumptions that new early childhood educators know nothing, need nothing, need to learn how things are done in the "real world," and are licensed and ready to go. Rather, beginning early childhood educators are viewed as ready to begin their work as an early childhood educator, as a contributing member of the workplace team.

In this model, communication is pivotal. Supportive administrative and supervisory practices are enabled, which allows time for the beginning early childhood educator to engage in observations of more experienced educators. Furthermore, the beginning early childhood educator is able to receive ongoing and relevant feedback on their practice. There is both time for planning with colleagues and summative evaluations, which allow the beginning early childhood educator to grow and fully develop into a professional. The entire staff team, including the beginning early childhood educator, has the opportunity for regular and sustained professional development, which is fully funded and supported by the government. The early childhood community of practice is deeply connected with both the local and provincial organizations representing Early Childhood Educators of British Columbia. Additionally, there are significant connections with the local early childhood education program at the nearest post-secondary institution, which assists the staff in remaining current. Speaking in the future tense, all of this is supported by the provincial and federal governments, who now adequately fund early childhood education programs.

Implications

In order for this model to be put into practice, there needs to be a mind shift, a change in the way we view the education and training of early childhood educators. Given that all eleven interview participants wanted a program of support for beginning early childhood educators, there are implications for the preparation of early childhood educators. For example, the training and education is not complete once the early childhood educator graduates after two to four semesters of post-secondary education. This may be the end to the formal training, but there should be a continuation of the necessary induction experiences through a community of practice. There needs to be a move toward a community of practice model where the workplace is responsible for the induction of early childhood educators. However, this is not possible when there is a high turnover of staff. Therefore, there needs to be stability within the staffing levels in every job site.

A change in how our society currently perceives the care and education of young children is necessary. It is time for us to recognize that we as a society are responsible for young children; parents are not solely responsible. There are economic reasons to support children and families, such as the increase in children's development and school success, and the workforce stability from which all citizens benefit. It has been argued that it is the early childhood educators who are subsidizing child care in British Columbia. Early childhood educators pay thousands of dollars to continue their education, knowing that even though they may be solely responsible for the care and education of eight preschoolers, they will make less than what they would if they worked at their local Tim Horton's coffee shop. Furthermore, it is assumed that early childhood educators will access professional development with their own money and on their own time, typically on weekends and evenings, and this is usually the case. Beginning early childhood educators in British Columbia perceive children and families as highly valued within the childcare setting, while the educators themselves are treated with little regard. This has to change.

In order to fully realize this model of best practice for the induction of beginning early childhood educators, leaders in the early childhood education field, such as ECEBC members, ECE Registry personnel, ECE faculty, and members of the ECE community must work together to design professional development opportunities for both experienced educators and beginning early childhood educators. Not all early childhood educators know how to collaborate, but this is something that can be learned. Experienced educators could have professional development opportunities where they can learn how to support beginning educators. Furthermore, experienced educators can learn how to work with beginning educators who may be entering the field with new knowledge, skills, or abilities. Instead of being threatened by this, as some participants of this study experienced, educators who have been in the field for a lengthy period of time can learn how to benefit from the beginning educator's experience.

Beginning educators could receive professional development related to advocating for their support needs. Participants of this study who did receive induction support often initiated the support. This is something that beginning early childhood educators can benefit from: how to access the support one needs. Furthermore, beginning early childhood educators and experienced educators could receive professional development on ways to develop communities of practice. However, as mentioned previously, the system requires additional funding to ensure staff have paid time for joint planning time, observations, feedback, professional development, and mentoring or peer support.

Further Research

More children than ever before participate in some kind of early learning program, making research into all things related to the care and education of children something that should be a priority (Nicholson & Reifel, 2011). Because so many early childhood educators leave the profession within the first five years, more research ought to be done on what helps in the retention of educators. This would provide gains for the following entities: children and families who benefit from continuity of care, staff and administrators who struggle with the realities of meeting government-imposed ratios of educators to children, and governments who stand to lose hundreds of thousands of dollars from money invested into post-secondary settings. In order to create a better system of care, we need to know what practices are most effective for retention.

This study looked specifically at new early childhood educators at work with five years or less of experience, following the statistic that in British Columbia we lose 50 percent of new educators in this time frame (Early Childhood Educators of British Columbia, 2012). Further research could compare and contrast the longevity of different groups. For example, does the level of education make a difference to the induction experience? Is an educator with a bachelor's degree more likely to stay in the field longer than an educator with a diploma? What other factors might be at play? Moreover, more research needs to be done with experienced educators, those who have been in the field longer than five years. Many experienced educators contacted the researcher, wanting to take part in this study, finding out that they were not eligible for participation. Of those who had personal contact with me, they shared an eagerness to take part in further research, believing they had something to offer. Generally speaking, early childhood educators are not seen to be a group that is interested in becoming involved in research, but this research study indicates there are many early childhood educators who wish to participate in research (Rodd, 2006).

ECEBC

The study's findings imply that it may be a good idea for the Early Childhood Educators of British Columbia (ECEBC) to look into having an accreditation process to support early childhood centers in having specific policies and procedures for supporting new educators. As one participant indicated, there are already strict rules in place for licensing, and administrators work hard to ensure compliance, so why not add induction activities to the list of things that a center must demonstrate they are providing?

Government Policy

Currently, the government has much to say about the physical environment of early childhood education programs, but very little to say about the staff in terms of professional development opportunities, remuneration for additional qualifications, and workplace practices to support beginning early childhood educators. For example, licensing officers visit childcare centers regularly to ensure the physical safety of the children, check the temperature of the fridge, and make sure all staff have licenses to practice, but more could be done to ensure that early childhood education programs have the means necessary to support the most valuable asset in this setting, the beginning early childhood educators. Many beginning early childhood educators in this study reported a lack of time for many of the induction activities. In fact, there is a reported lack of time for planning and preparation of learning experiences for children. Much of this comes back to a lack of funding and a lack of government policy supporting the work of early childhood educators. This is in sharp contrast to public school teachers who enjoy such benefits as regular paid professional development days.

Post-Secondary Institutions

A majority of beginning early childhood educators in this study reported they felt unprepared and overwhelmed for the work as an early childhood educator. There were many factors for this, including the vast difference in experience from being in practicum to being a staff member. Clearly, there is much that can be done when it comes to supporting early childhood education students prior to the completion of their program. For example, faculty in post-secondary early childhood education programs should work at ensuring students understand the realities of the field. The long hours and lack of induction activities should be discussed in a way to inform and help students to problem solve. Further to this, early childhood education faculties have a duty to work with community educators to support beginning early childhood educators. To this end, professional development can be offered to support sponsor educators who work with beginning early childhood educators. Faculty could foster the idea of communities of practice by introducing the concept to the early childhood education curriculum and by conducting research on how to develop and sustain communities of practice.

Limitations

Some beginning early childhood educators may have been unwilling to participate or they may have been reluctant to share openly about challenges faced in the first year of their practice. Moreover, early childhood educators teaching in their first year may not have wanted to get involved in this study and this may be due to many factors including lack of interest in the study, lack of time (due to survival mode), and/or perceived beliefs that what they have to say will not make a difference. In their study on teacher induction in New Zealand, Aitken et al. (2008) reported that some participants may have "felt some reluctance or fear about their own teacher registration process being scrutinized by the researcher, or were reluctant to say something critical about the support they received from their mentor teacher or centre" (p. 22), and participants in this study may have been unwilling to share openly for the same reasons. It was imperative that I earn the trust of the participants by following ethical procedures throughout the research process and by assuring participants of anonymity. Additionally, Aitken et al. reported an "inability to use observation as a means of gathering data" as a possible limitation, and I may face the same limitation as I relied on participant reports and not direct observations. These limitations may have been a problem for me had I been unable to recruit participants. Additionally, if I was unable to earn the trust of the participants involved in the semi-structured interviews, then the data may not have been accurate.

There are at least three additional possible limitations of this study. First, the quantitative data gathered through the use of an online questionnaire may be biased due to the fact that participants took part through a self-selection process. For example, it is probable that those who took part were either beginning early childhood educators who were doing quite well in their first year or were doing rather poorly. Additionally, the data from the semi-structured interviews may not be fully accurate as it is possible that what participants shared is different from what they do in practice. Finally, relative to the number of beginning early childhood educators in British Columbia, this study involved a small number. Thus, the findings, though useful for this particular context, are not generalizable.

The findings from this study indicate that beginning early childhood educators in British Columbia have both a need and a desire for induction support in the form of mentoring or peer support, observations, feedback, and professional development. The induction support received is haphazard, meaning early childhood educators in British Columbia are not assured of receiving what they need in their induction year. That said, those who do receive support report assistance received from coworkers, supervisors, and administrators. The theory of educator development by Katz (1972) was discussed, with an emphasis on how the findings from this study add to this theory.

The Doan model of best practice for the induction of beginning early childhood educators suggests a move toward viewing early childhood education workplaces as "communities of practice," a term used by Lave and Wenger (1991). In order to bring this concept into fruition, much will be required, including the involvement of governments, post-secondary institutions, and ECEBC (the provincial organization representing early childhood educators in British Columbia). Recommendations for further research have been presented. Despite challenges such as inconsistent induction support, beginning early childhood educators in British Columbia are deeply satisfied with their work, and this is reason for optimism.

8

Theories and New Directions in Early Childhood Education

Involving Early Childhood Educators in Research on Educators

There has been a gap in the literature when it comes to understanding the needs and experiences of beginning early childhood educators (Neuman, Josephson, & Chua, 2015; Mahmood, 2012). When thinking about creating programs of support for early childhood educators, it is important to find out what educators want in the first place. If we are to make a difference in the lives of early childhood educators, it is my belief that we must involve them in research as active participants. In my work, I have sought to position myself as working *with* educators, joining them, learning from them, and creating programs of support, based on what they have told me they want. My approach has been to seek out the perspectives of educators. This is an approach that positions early childhood educators as knowing, having critical experiences and perceptions that can shed light into the issues of recruitment and retention.

Programs of Support for Early Childhood Educators: An Iterative Process

In this book, I have described the needs and experiences of beginning early childhood educators in British Columbia. All of this is based on research with educators who were eager to share their experiences. Taking this research, and specifically new educators' desire for an induction program, I started the *Induction Support Pilot Project*, which took place in the interior of British Columbia. This project included peer mentoring, participation in a community of practice, access to professional development, opportunities to meet with ECE faculty, online support through a WordPress site, and visits to early learning programs. Results from this project include a greater awareness of the value of mentoring, a deeper connection to the early childhood education community, and an increase in knowledge and skills (Doan, 2018). One educator shared, *"One of the reasons why ECEs burn out so quickly [is that] they are overworked and they are not valued. And I think that peer mentorship will [help]. Having those constant valuing comments and support—it would sustain us a lot in this field"* (Doan, 2018, p. 15).

From there a Peer Mentoring Project was launched in 2017. This was based on the pilot project but included a greater emphasis on peer mentoring. In the previous project, participants had been introduced and then left to partner up with someone, on their own. Feedback from participants was that the process was not helpful, and the preference was to be paired up. In addition, while an email list was used for communication, its usefulness was limited, and participants asked for a private group to be set up on Facebook, as there was not enough time to be accessing and responding to email. Educators specifically liked the fact that they would be able to access Facebook on their phones, while on short breaks, and they would receive notifications if there were any new posts, and so on.

In 2019, the Peer Mentoring Program received $750,000, which allowed us to expand across the province of British Columbia, to 17 peer mentoring communities of practice, with 20 facilitators and 200 early childhood educators. Building on what was done previously in the pilot project, the purpose of the program was to support the ongoing professional development needs of beginning and experienced early childhood educators. Specifically, we hoped to slow the numbers of educators who leave the field. Additionally, we aimed to build the capacity of early childhood educators, support their ongoing professional identity development, and increase their levels of educator efficacy and their confidence in their own abilities. We used a peer mentoring model, as new early childhood educators acknowledged that they had value and have things to contribute in a mentoring relationship. By using a nonhierarchical approach, we hoped that learning would occur for both new and experienced early childhood educators.

Individual peer mentoring communities of practice had autonomy about what they chose to do, in terms of professional development, and the hope was that this would (1) enable educators to identify and focus on their own motivations and/or interests and (2) encourage educator efficacy. The structure was purposely left open and flexible, to allow individual communities of practice to determine what their interests were. Through this program, educators were able to: share perspectives, develop professional friendships, learn from and reflect with each other, support each other, and feel valued and heard. The structure of the project brought educators together, breaking down barriers, and uniting educators together with a common purpose and vision. Educators highlighted that having someone who listens to them, who understands them, and who supports their practice as a fellow early childhood education professional through this web of connection was self-care itself, which was important for their well-being. One educator shared:

> *I found out about the Peer Mentoring Program at a crucial point in my career. . . . I had just reached the five year mark working as an early childhood educator . . . and I was beginning to feel the effects of burnout, [stagnancy], and was unsure where I was heading in my career path. . . . I remember walking into the room for the first time after being invited to be part of this research project. . . . I didn't realize how much I needed another educator to connect with, and feel inspired by until I met with my peer-mentor the first time.* (Doan et al., 2021, p. 16)

Benefits of a Peer Mentoring Community of Practice

The structure of the peer mentoring community of practice is set up in a way that intentionally allows educators time to stop, think, and reflect. This happens within the monthly group meetings and within the weekly times with their peer-mentor pair. Early childhood educators within the British Columbia context have very little time during their workday to sit, to be, and to reflect with one another, and I suspect this is the same for other jurisdictions. The typical day is one that is marked with busyness as each educator is responsible for eight three-to five-year-old children. Add to this the impact of being short-staffed, as well as working alongside educators who are not fully qualified, and these factors influence the stress that educators experience daily in their work. One educator shared this reflection from a conversation with her peer mentor: "*Discussed challenges setting boundaries with coworkers, shortage of qualified staff (e.g. when staff is not well, they can't go home because they know there are no other staff to call in). Talked about long hours, burnout, the mental load on educators, constant change and inconsistency of staff*" (Doan & Jang, 2020).

    I have both led peer mentoring communities of practice and visited sixteen across our province, and I have witnessed the impact that a prepared environment can make. Imagine an early childhood educator walking into a room that includes a circle of chairs, light snacks or a meal, and a caring facilitator. For early childhood educators who are usually the ones responsible for creating spaces and environments for children, the impact can be huge. One educator and participant described her time this way: "*Our time together 'filled my cup', each sip of tea warming my insides. When my tea mug was physically empty, I felt refreshed mentally.*" A facilitator shared this reflection: "*Reflecting on our meeting, I was struck by the fact we had created a safe, secure base over the past months together, from which to travel bravely forth with new questions, inquiries, and ways to problematize the underlying structure of areas in our practice that need deeper critical reflection*" (Doan & Jang, 2020).

Belonging in a Peer Mentoring Community of Practice

I have found Brene Brown's research on the differences between belonging and fitting in to be profound. Brown wrote: "Fitting in is about assessing a situation and becoming who you need to be to be accepted. Belonging, on the other hand, doesn't require us to change who we are; it requires us to *be* who we are" (2010, p. 25). In a Peer Mentoring Community of Practice, educators are welcomed as they are. As shared previously, a core belief of our program is that we believe that educators have worth, knowledge, and critical expertise. Our facilitators are committed to supporting relationship building between the educators, with an aim to create a safe place where each person feels valued and knows they are cared for. From this environment, early childhood educators feel comfortable to share openly, their struggles, questions, joys, and dreams. They can be vulnerable because they know they are with people who genuinely care and want the best for them. One early childhood educator described their experience in the Peer Mentoring Program this way: "*When you come together, it's creating a space for vulnerability, which I think is important . . . you can't really share that you might have a different opinion from someone else if you don't feel safe being vulnerable*" (Doan & Jang, 2020).

Future Programs of Support

The research shared in this book as well as in this chapter can be used as a baseline for future Peer Mentoring Programs for early childhood educators. Having traveled internationally to present on this work, I know there is interest internationally in ways to support early childhood educators. There is a recognition worldwide of the current crisis in early learning and child care, where we are facing huge shortages of early childhood educators. Government officials, policymakers, and early learning and care leaders are seeing the need for ongoing programs of support for early childhood educators, such as the Peer Mentoring Program for Early Childhood Educators in British Columbia. Researchers have found that professional development that is government funded can help to ensure quality programs and greater educator retention (Totenhagen et al., 2016).

Critical Pieces to Consider When Setting Up Programs of Support for Early Childhood Educators

Listen to the Educators

Listen to the educators; position them as experts. They are after all the people with lived experience. Build programs of support *with* early childhood educators. This is truly a constructivist approach, where multiple perspectives are valued, and it is understood that building together is the way to go. Conduct a pilot project in your local area, with local early childhood educators. Build on this. Find out what worked well and what can be changed for the next time. There is greater buy-in to a program when educators see educators taking part. When you can show the impact on educators, and you use educators' own words, that makes a huge difference. One educator shared her experience in the Peer Mentoring Program for Early Childhood Educators in BC: "*I find that I look forward to these meetings and feel in a way refreshed after having them. There is something almost therapeutic about being able to talk to someone who understands you and your job*" (Doan & Jang, 2020).

Confidentiality

From the very beginning, early childhood educators in the Peer Mentoring Programs that I have set up have signed an agreement of confidentiality. This is a recognition that what is shared in the individual peer mentoring pair meetings, and in the community of practice meetings, is kept safe within the pair or group. Educators have described their community of practice as a "safe space to share their vulnerabilities, since, for most of them, there were no employer-employee relationships within the group, and they knew that confidentiality was at the core of their participation in this project" (Doan & Jang, 2020). Early childhood educators shared this about their experiences with confidentiality: "*I was comfortable sharing things that I wouldn't share with anybody else about what is happening at my workplace and the stress of owning my own business in the busy center . . . so, having that confidentiality was huge*"; "*When you come together, it's creating a space for vulnerability, which I think is important. . . . You can't really share that you might have a different opinion from someone if you don't feel safe being vulnerable*"; and "*We kind of created a safe environment, I think, that we both share our vulnerability, you know, throughout our day and our daily practice. And then, having that space to bounce off some ideas was very supportive for me*" (Doan & Jang, 2020).

Multiple Ways to Participate

When I initially researched mentoring programs, my main learning was that there was not a "one-size-fits-all" kind of program. This led me to the conclusion that a one-pronged approach such as mentor to mentee, was not going to be as effective as a more multidimensional model. See Figure 8.0, What makes a Peer Mentoring Program successful.

The approach was peer mentor to peer mentor (educator to educator), within a community of practice. More detail on this is provided later. Professional development took place within the community of practice. Visits to early learning programs were another facet of the program. All of these aspects came out of the induction research I conducted as well as pilot peer mentoring projects. For example, educators in my initial research had shared their perspectives on the

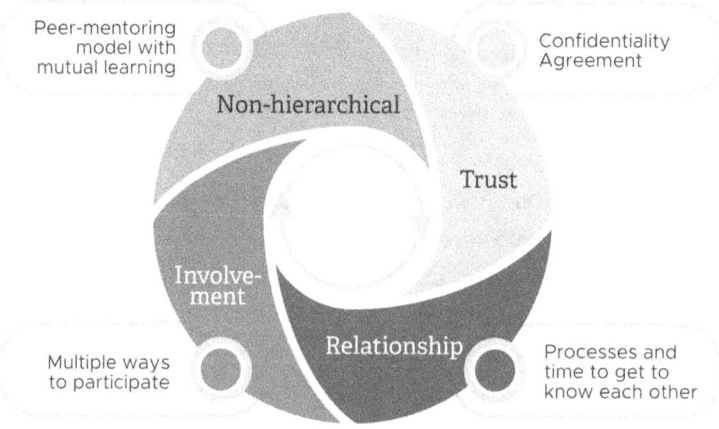

Figure 8.0 What makes a Peer Mentoring Program successful. © Laura K. Doan.

importance of seeing many different programs. The lived experience of many educators is that due to the shortage of early childhood educators, they are offered positions while they are still in the post-secondary system, completing their practica. This can result in educators getting into one program through a practica course and then staying on through paid employment. This is not bad per se, but educators in my induction study thought it was important for new educators to have the opportunity to see a variety of early learning programs to experience how varied educational approaches and philosophical orientations can be. I see the value of this, as I think it is important for early childhood educators to know that there is a lot of variety within the early learning field, and if one is not finding a particular early learning program a good fit, due to philosophy, for example, there are other choices to consider.

This, however, can be very challenging for early childhood educators to actually consider. Having taught in the post-secondary system for twenty-three years, I have met hundreds of educators. One thing I have noticed generally is a sense of deep loyalty to the children, families, and educators within an early learning program. This can be the reason why some educators stay, and some go. Within a peer mentoring community of practice, educators can find mutual understanding and support, and this can help them to consider the possibility of leaving one position, for the purpose of finding another that is a better fit and/or one where they are treated more equitably.

Nonhierarchical Approach

As I have mentioned in the previous chapters, new early childhood educators who took part in the research on their needs and experiences in the first five years of work indicated that, while they had specific needs, they also had things to share and contribute. New early childhood educators want to feel valued on a team, as they have expertise and knowledge to share. For these reasons, I have opted for a nonhierarchical approach to both the peer mentoring and how the community of practice operates.

Research-Informed Background for the Nonhierarchical Approach

As I delved into the induction research and heard about experiences such as Emma who was told she wasn't supposed to be completing pedagogical narrations at the workplace as it was "not something we do here," I wondered about the experiences for educators who have been in the early learning and care field for a long time. One research study out of Prince Edward Island, in Canada, found that experienced early childhood educators felt confident as a professional while also dealing with imposter syndrome (Roach O'Keefe, Hooper, & Jakubiec, 2019). One educator shared,

> *Well, in college we were taught you pick your theme and we had to plan a whole week. . . . Then the [early learning] framework came into place ad it was like no, you go with the interests of the children, so then I was like, what? What do we do with all this planning we were taught to do? So there was kind of a period of confusion. It was like, do I keep my themes, do I keep doing what I was doing, or we thought we had to stop that and observe the kids and see what they like to do, and we didn't really understand the framework, we didn't know what to do with it! So it was very confusing. . . . Like, lost.* (Roach O'Keefe, Hooper, & Jakubiec, 2019, p. 28)

Take a moment to let that sink in. You are a trained early childhood educator, you have completed post-secondary education, but now, some twenty-five years later, you find yourself being asked to work in ways that you have not previously learned. The contrast for some is huge and can look like: being taught to create weekly themes to now moving to an emergent curriculum, where you follow the child's interests (as we saw with the previous quotation). This can also look like moving from anecdotal and running records of children, where you intentionally keep your own thoughts and voice out of the observation, to a pedagogical narration (or documentation) where you intentionally bring in not just your own voice, but multiple voices, including children, families, and other educators. Talk about a mind shift or a pivot, and yet, is this acknowledged as one? No wonder we have such issues in recruitment and retention.

While my induction research focused on the needs and experiences of beginning early childhood educators, I became aware of the need for research and support for experienced educators as well. This is why the Peer Mentoring Program is not simply for new educators but instead for all early childhood educators, both new and experienced. For this reason, I have gone with a nonhierarchical model, a peer-to-peer mentoring model, as opposed to the traditional mentor-mentee or mentor-protégé model. In the latter model, it positions the experienced educator as the expert and the new educator who needs the support. In contrast, the peer-to-peer model recognizes that both educators have experience, both have things to learn, and both can support the other. Neither one is viewed as the expert, the one with all the answers. And while the experienced educator likely brings a depth of knowledge and understanding of the role of the early childhood educator, the new educator brings new knowledge and understandings that the experienced educator may not be familiar with, and this is okay. For example, in my context where the British Columbia Early Learning Framework exists, early childhood education students learn how to create pedagogical narrations, or learning stories based on children's involvement in early learning programs. However, for many experienced early childhood educators, this is not something they are familiar with. In a situation like this, positioning the experienced educator as the "expert" seems to me like a setup. In contrast, in the peer-to-peer model, there is room and space for educators to explore concepts like pedagogical narrations, the complexity of working with families, and interpersonal relations at work, together, in a nonhierarchical fashion, and learning can occur for both peers, regardless of their level of experience. Here is an example of a reflection from a peer mentor who was learning about pedagogical narrations (PNs):

> *Today's focus was about Pedagogical Narrations (PNs). . . . We had some printed examples to refer to, as well [our facilitator] shared ideas of different digital formats that could be used. This discussion was greatly received as many of us are unsure, unaware, or unpracticed at preparing PNs, but we see value in them and want to incorporate them into our daily practice for recording and future reflection with the children at work.* (Doan & Jang, 2020)

This example is one that highlights adult learning theory, where educators are met in their time of need and motivation (Knowles, Holton, & Swanson, 2012), and builds educator efficacy (Bandura, 1997).

Using the Community of Practice Model

Within a community of practice, each person has a voice and is important. Each person can contribute, no matter what their experience is. In describing the value of communities of practice, Wenger, McDermott, and Snyder (2002), shared, "their greatest value lies in intangible outcomes, such as the relationships they build among people, the sense of belonging they create, the spirit of inquiry they generate, and the professional confidence and identity they confer to their members" (p. 14). Within a community of practice, model, each voice is valued.

The individual peer mentoring community of practice groups mentioned previously, meet face-to-face, once a month. Some groups have opted for a virtual meeting space, but feedback thus far is that while this does create opportunities to meet, it is a much different environment than the face-to-face one. Being in the same physical room as someone else allows for educators to pick up on nuances, such as body language, tone of voice, and educators reporting feeling more comfortable sharing within the face-to-face environment.

Time spent within the peer mentoring community of practice is viewed as professional development. The meetings were for building relationships and learning from one another. This may have included a guest speaker, depending on the group's interest, and each group in our study received funds for this purpose. By having the professional development take place within the community of practice, educators have time to process the material, revisit it and continue the dialogue, as well as exploration, in future group meetings, as well as in their weekly pair meetings. One of our facilitators described it this way: *"It's not just a one time workshop. It's a community of practice, we come together, and we build that relationship. And then we form our professional identity together. And I think in our group we even talk about just today about advocacy. And that's so important in our field right now"* (Doan, 2022, p. 17).

Each group had one or two facilitators, who led the group, based on their interests. The approach to professional development is one of from the ground up versus a top-down approach. In this case, the educators are the ones who choose what area they would like to focus on, and the facilitator can support them in that. This is a tangible way of both valuing educators and recognizing them as experts on what they need to continue their growth as professionals. This also recognizes and reinforces the theory that becoming an educator, a professional, takes time, and it requires access to ongoing support. Further to this, an intention behind the structure of the program is for educators to raise their levels of educator efficacy and their confidence in themselves. This can happen within a peer mentoring community of practice when educators feel valued by one another as well as the facilitator. Furthermore, when educators are listened to and invited to share their perspectives, they have the opportunity to feel heard, and to be seen as worthy of sharing an opinion or thought. One educator described her time this way: *"Feeling heard, acknowledged and valued was so meaningful! I would love for this project to continue and to be part of it"* (Doan & Jang, 2020).

The top six topics that educators wanted to explore with the peer mentoring communities of practice in 2021–2, were: Reflective Practice, Educator Health and Well-being; ECEBC Code of Ethics; Indigenous Perspectives and Worldviews; Early Learning and Child Care Legislation in BC; and Providing Healthy Child Care Environments during Covid-19. Here are two reflections from educators about the professional development that they took part in: *"we participated in a workshop on communication, difficult conversations and how to be more courageous, vulnerable, transparent, compassionate and kind human beings*"; and "*Today's meeting was a workshop on emotional intelligence and values. . . . Today's meeting helped me to reflect on my true and honest values, and narrow down my most important values. I want to take what I've learned here, to focus on one change I can make, and stick with*" (Doan & Jang, 2020). Because the professional development is based on what educators want, this means it can be relevant, timely, and of interest, and this fits within Knowles' adult learning theory (2012), which emphasizes the importance of meeting learners where they are at, at the time of their motivation.

Partnerships: What to Consider

When it comes to partnerships, it is important to think strategically. Who is connected to educators in your community? Who does it make sense to partner with? Who in your community has shared goals with you re: supporting educators? Who can you partner with to make a difference?

In my circumstance, coming from a post-secondary context, it has made sense for me to partner with the local and provincial professional associations of early childhood educators of BC. Where are you situated in your work? This is important to consider, as you likely need others in order to make a significant difference and/or impact. The Peer Mentoring Program for Early Childhood Educators in BC has included many partners: the post-secondary system, the provincial professional association ECEBC, and the Ministry of Education and Child Care. Going a bit deeper into the relationships and partners, there are more at play. The facilitators come from across the province and work in programs directly with children as well as post-secondary institutions, and other organizations that support early childhood educators, such as the Child Care Resource and Referral Programs.

Sharing Your Results

If you want to make an impact, you need to share what you are doing. This can be done at multiple levels: local, regional, provincial, national, and international. At the local level, who can you share with? Is there an opportunity to share a presentation and/or workshop with early childhood educators, administrators, and/or other stakeholders?

If you are fortunate to have funding, it is critical that your funders hear about the success of your work. This is especially important when the work you are doing fits very well with their mandate. When you meet your goals, you help them to achieve the mandate they have, and this can result in both new awareness of what is possible in supporting early childhood educators and the assurance that you will receive ongoing funding. A graphic designer can help you to communicate your results in a way that will draw people to them. Infographics are a great way to share the story of your program.

Does your professional association have a journal that you could contribute to? This is another great way to share information about your program. You can invite stakeholders, as well as participants to contribute, which helps to show the depth and breadth of the impact. Pay attention to the audience you are trying to reach. This can help you to avoid language and/or a writing style that may get in the way of what you want to convey.

Research with Early Childhood Educators Is Powerful

When we work together with early childhood educators on research projects, we turn the tides of the way things are done. Educators have voice and full participation, as well as agency. They are actors in the narrative and can give direction to the future. When we bring those voices forward, into the open, we shed light onto the issues facing early childhood educators, and we have the opportunity to advocate for their ongoing support. I think this is important to consider when designing research studies with early childhood educators.

Qualitative researchers seek to study a phenomenon by conducting research in natural settings (Denzin & Lincoln, 2005). Furthermore, those involved in qualitative research believe that reality is socially constructed, that researchers have a relationship with what is being studied, and that investigation is shaped by limitations in the circumstance. Qualitative researchers believe they can acquire "rich descriptions of the social world" (p. 12), and this is one reason this study is qualitative dominant. As the purpose of this research was to uncover early childhood educators' beliefs, understandings, and perspectives on the professional development needs of novice early childhood educators, I tended toward the use of the constructivist end of the paradigmatic orientation. A constructivist perspective means the ontology or assertions about what knowledge is involves "local and specific co-constructed realities" (Guba & Lincoln, 2005, p. 194), and I believed this was the best approach for studying the phenomenon of induction experiences of beginning early childhood educators. Additionally, context is valued as I believed the participants' context played a pivotal role in shaping their induction experiences. The epistemology or philosophical stance regarding "how we know what we know" (Bloomberg & Volpe, 2012, p. 28) is subjectivist with results that are co-created by the participants and the researcher. A fundamental assumption of constructivism is that "reality is socially constructed" with individuals creating their own meaning of their personal experience (Bloomberg & Volpe, 2012, p. 29). As the researcher, it was my responsibility to appreciate the multiple realities presented from the participants' perceptions.

Why Not Simply Raise the Wages of Early Childhood Educators?

I once had a potential funder ask me this question and found that it was a good question to respond to. First, regarding the question of do we put money into increasing wages or do we support projects that have an impact on the workplace, I don't see this as an either/or. I see the support to early childhood educators through projects like the Peer Mentoring Program, and the advocacy for increased wages as initiatives that go hand in hand. They support each other. However, if we are to look at just one or the other, simply having a higher wage does not necessarily lead to greater support in the workplace. Having a higher income does not mean that educators now know how to support each other, how to work well together, and how to successfully induct new educators. While a raise in the salary of educators may help in the recruitment in the short term, it will not necessarily result in educators staying in the field for longer periods of time.

A further thought on this is that ultimately we also want to have an impact on children and families, and this can happen through peer mentoring communities of practice. When educators are able to access timely professional development that enables their ability to support children and families, then is an impact then on quality.

In addition, I think that by gathering educators together to have opportunities to share their stories, to be heard, to make action plans, and to problem solve also helps educators to actually mobilize in order to make change and advocate for higher wages. I see the Peer Mentoring Program itself supporting everything to do with wage, but in an indirect way. If we were to simply raise the wages,

I do not believe that would have the impact that this program has on educator confidence or educator efficacy. I am reminded of the educator who shared that she was in a unionized position, so she was getting a higher wage, and in a protected position, and her unionized supervisor told her, "*We don't do this here,*" as in we do not do pedagogical narrations (learning stories), we do not do this innovative work. She then started doing the pedagogical narrations on her break, but she was told, "*your break is your break.*" At the end of the day, she told me, if she cannot do innovative work, she will leave the field. It is not just about the wage.

Raising wages is important, but it does not result in the kind of learning and benefit that can come from peer mentoring through a community of practice.

> Sharing knowledge is not about giving people something, or getting something from them. That is only valid for information sharing. Sharing knowledge occurs when people are genuinely interested in helping one another develop new capacities for action; it is about creating learning processes. (Senge, 2022)

Other Programs of Support

It is heartening to see the number of early childhood education programs that are recognizing and utilizing the strategies of peer mentoring and communities of practice. In British Columbia, the Early Childhood Educators of British Columbia (ECEBC) has partnered with the British Columbia Aboriginal Child Care Society (BCACCS), Indigenous Elders, Dr. Enid Elliot, Ms. Karolyn Hendra, and others to create the Learning On the Land Together (LOT) Program. This program utilizes a community of practice model, as well as a mentoring approach, which supports small group and individual learning within a supportive small group. The mentoring model is based on the Peer Mentoring Program for Early Childhood Educators in BC. This includes a mentor who works with a small group of educators, supporting them as they go through the modules. The purpose of the program is to build educator capacity and confidence in programming in the outdoor space, and the leaders of the program have recognized that embedding mentoring into the learning process is a powerful tool to ensure this happens (Early Childhood Educators of British Columbia, 2022a).

In Ontario, on the other side of Canada, there are two programs using the community of practice model. One operates out of the Association of Early

Childhood Educators of Ontario (AECEO). The focus of these communities of practice is around advocacy, and with other communities of practice, educators take the lead in terms of what that looks like. Currently, there are nine communities of practice: some are regionally based and some are focused around a particular content area, such as "Newcomer Services" or "Community of Black ECEs" (Association of Early Childhood Educators of Ontario, 2022). This is how they describe the communities of practice:

> A Community of Practice (CoP) is a regional or allied collective that acts as an extension of the provincial body and collaborates with the AECEO to provide access to the decent work and professional pay project across the province. These CoPs are self-determined learning groups that connect folks to supports, resources, and shared experiences to strengthen a unified early years workforce (Association of Early Childhood Educators of Ontario, 2022).

Another program in Ontario is piloting a Peer Mentoring Program specifically for Indigenous early childhood educators (M. Taylor-Leonhardi, personal communication, June 28, 2022). This program aims to support Indigenous early childhood educators who are geographically isolated and apart from one another.

In Ireland, Mary Immaculate College is offering a Level 8 Special Purpose Certificate in Professional Mentoring for Early Childhood Practice (Mary Immaculate College, 2022). This 15-credit module is led by Dr. Mary Moloney aims to benefit early childhood educators and managers by: "Focusing upon empowering existing ECEC staff to mentor early childhood students undertaking practical placements while engaging in their undergraduate degree programme; Strengthen the capacity of existing ECEC staff to support the professional formation of undergraduate students" (Mary Immaculate College, 2022). In addition, it is hoped that there will be benefits to early childhood education students "by enhancing the quality of their experience during practical placement, enabling them to be better prepared for the demands of their professional role and better placed to enter the workforce as professional educators" (Mary Immaculate College, 2022).

In addition to the program running out of Mary Immaculate College, researchers Dr. Alison Moore and Ms. Marcella Towler from the University of Cork have recently completed a pilot community of practice for students, university staff, and placement mentors (Moore & Towler, 2022). This pilot project created a space and a structure to create meaningful engagement, collaboration, capacity building, and identifying and sharing best practice.

As with the Peer Mentoring Program for Early Childhood Educators in BC, this pilot project valued each member and recognized the experience that each member brought to the community. Another program out of Ireland has just completed the pilot stage. This is a program that uses the community of practice model that has been shared throughout this book. At this stage, Dr. Margaret Kernan, the primary researcher, has shared that participants in the community of practice have a "desire to increase natural materials and sensory play outdoors; increase parental engagements; enhance indoor-outdoor connections and provide outdoor play for under 3s in all weathers" (Kernan, Casey, & Dowdall, 2022).

In Scotland, where there is an increasing emphasis on learning outdoors, initiatives to support early childhood educators in this new way of programming are taking place. For example, working with the Aberdeen City Council, Dr. Elizabeth Henderson worked with local educators to set up a community of practice for educators who were interested in learning more about how to utilize the outdoor space in early learning programs. Henderson and Beaton wrote:

> Previous experience at expanding our outdoor provision in Aberdeen has had limited impact, highlighting several systemic challenges, namely: practitioner insecurity about new practices; lack of knowledge; too few experienced staff to accompany and role-model new practices for others; lack of opportunity for immersion in outdoor settings to engage with enthusiastic, informed and motivated others; lack of understanding of outdoor child-centered pedagogies, lack of understanding of the importance of outdoor practices for children's development. (2020)

Recognizing these challenges, under Dr. Henderson's facilitation, the group utilized the community of practice method to support one another in learning and taking risks in going outdoors with young children. Dr. Henderson was successful in receiving funding through the Erasmus Foundation, which enabled this community of practice to travel to Germany and Spain, for the purpose of experiencing outdoor settings, as well as receiving training on how to initiate and develop these programs (Beaton & Henderson, 2020). The goal of the community of practice was to "create a strong peer-group to emerge that go on to become Champions of Practice, with enhanced skills, knowledge and understanding of outdoor nursery pedagogies" (Beaton & Henderson, 2020).

In this chapter I discussed many examples of programs of support for early childhood educators. The Peer Mentoring Program for Early Childhood

Educators in BC builds directly from the research in this book, and it is an excellent example of what can happen when researchers work directly with early childhood educators. From looking at programs across Canada, as well as in Ireland and Scotland, we can see the power that exists within communities of practice, as well as peer mentoring. These are excellent strategies to employ when it comes to supporting early childhood educators in their own development as educators, as well as implementing new curriculum and/or approaches. Never underestimate the power of a group of early childhood educators coming together, with the common goal of lifting one another up.

Conclusion

Communities of practice is a powerful approach to supporting early childhood educators from induction and throughout their career. It is in direct contrast to the feelings of isolation and/or the "sink or swim" approach that many new early childhood educators face and instead it brings early childhood educators together. This approach shines the light on the expertise within the group, values each member, and contrasts with a top-down model of professional development that is often seen in early learning and care. Peer mentoring within a community of practice creates a space for educators to come together for mutual support, reflection on practice, and critical conversations. Within this environment, educators have opportunities to think about their place within the world, share insight with each other, and contemplate pedagogical approaches in early learning. The peer mentoring within a community of practice framework utilizes a nonhierarchical approach, where educators are viewed as knowing and as expert within their own practice. In contrast to the one-time workshop, where a list of objectives are shared, this is revolutionary. The facilitator of a peer mentoring community of practice does not provide the content, but she or he looks to the educators for direction of the content.

Early childhood educators who took part in a Peer Mentoring Community of Practice described their experience this way: "*I would describe the peer mentoring program as going home, being with a group of people who create safe spaces, and allow you to be the best version of yourself. It's been a valuable tool.*"; "*I think the peer mentoring program can help with burnout and can help with stress and support when there's not always much support.*"; "*As an early childhood educator, the peer mentoring program has been wonderful for me, because I retired last year, but yet my heart hasn't retired. So, I definitely wanted to still be a part of a community of educators. So being a part of the peer mentoring program enabled me to have a partner that was in the field a lot less time that I was. And so we developed a wonderful relationship and shared the struggles, the achievements, the accomplishment, of being the best we can be with the children in our care*" (Doan, 2022, p. 17). What a contrast these quotations are to the educators who were left to figure things out on their own.

Revisiting the four theories we looked at the beginning, how might we support educator efficacy? How can we meet educators at their time of need and motivation (adult learning theory)? How might we support educators as they make the transition into the role of an early childhood educator, knowing that this transition takes time (professional identity development)? And how can we be part of bringing early childhood educators together within a community of practice, a space where educators can find belonging, shared understanding, and collective wisdom (communities of practice)? Look to the educators in your local context, be that your city, province, or country. What are their experiences? How might you bring the early childhood educators together in your area, to learn from and provide a space for them to connect, grow, and learn from one another?

Life Preserver

Together we flounder in a wide sea—struggling to keep our heads above water. But then, through connection, someone throws us a life preserver and we hang on for dear life. After a while a boat comes along and we all climb aboard. And soon we are all rowing together—stronger and more purposeful.

That is what the peer mentoring project has done for me—connecting me with a partner who was my life preserver, then integrating me into a group of inspiring educators, who support each other without question. And that is a gift. Imagine the possibilities of pods of educators around the Province, gaining strength with each new group member. Realizing that we are not alone and that we share the same struggles. Wouldn't it be wonderful if every educator had this opportunity—and imagine the effect this would have on recruitment and retention. I certainly hope this is the case.

Charlene

Figure 9.0 Life preserver. © Charlene Gray.

In this book I have shared the voices of beginning early childhood educators. Their perspectives have been rich with experience, insight, and wisdom. How do we move forward with this? Countries across the world are seeing the impact of early learning and care on children, families, and communities, and many are working toward sustainable and equitable workplaces for early childhood educators. Imagine workplaces where early childhood educators not only survive but thrive, where retention and recruitment are no longer a necessary focus. An environment where early childhood educators who are passionate about making an impact on children, families, and the local community are recognized for their skill and expertise, and are remunerated accordingly—where beginning early childhood educators receive induction support through peer mentoring, access to professional development, observations, and feedback. An environment where early childhood educators are valued and can count on receiving ongoing professional development and the opportunity to participate in a peer mentoring community of practice, for mutual support, learning, and connection. Imagine what would happen if all of this was in place (Figure 9.0).

References

Ahmad, J., Saffardin, S. F., & Teoh, K. B. (2020). How does job demands and job resources affect work engagement towards burnout? The case of Penang preschool. *International Journal of Psychosocial Rehabilitation, 24*(02), 1888–1895. https://www.sentral.edu.my/wp-content/uploads/2020/10/How-Does-Job-Demands-and-Job-Resources-Affect-Work-Engagement-Towards-Burnout-The-Case-of-Penang-Pres_IJoPR.pdf

Aitken, H., Ferguson, P. B., McGrath, F., Piggot-Irvine, E., & Ritchie, J. (2008). *Learning to teach: Success case studies of teacher induction in Aotearoa.* New Zealand: New Zealand Teachers Council.

Aitken, R. & Harford, J. (2010). Induction needs of a group of teachers at different career stages in a school in the Republic of Ireland: Challenges and expectations. *Teaching and Teacher Education, 27*, 350–356.

Association of Early Childhood Educators of Ontario (2022). Communities of practice. Association of Early Childhood Educators of Ontario. https://www.aeceo.ca/communities_of_practice

Bandura, A. (1993). Perceived self-efficacy in cognitive development and functioning. *Educational Psychologist 28*(2), 117–148.

Bandura, A. (1997). *Self-efficacy: The exercise of control.* United States of America: W.H. Freeman and Company.

Bandura, A. (2001). Social cognitive theory: An agentic perspective. *Annual Review Psychology, 51*(1), 1–26.

Beaton, L. & Henderson, E. (2020). Erasmus programme travel out with UK-April 2020. Aberdeen City Council. https://committees.aberdeencity.gov.uk/documents/s106053/Erasmus%20Travel.pdf

Bella, J. & Bloom, P. J. (2003). *Zoom: The impact of early childhood leadership training on role perceptions, job performance, and career decisions.* Wheeling: The Centre for Early Childhood Leadership.

Bellm, D. & Whitebrook, M. (1996). Mentoring for early childhood teachers and providers: Building upon and extending tradition. *Young Children 52*(1), 59–64.

Blochlinger, O. R. & Bauer, G. F. (2018). Correlates of burnout symptoms among child care teachers. A multilevel modeling approach. *European Early Childhood Education Research Association Journal, 26*(1), 7–25. http://doi.org/10.1080/1350293X.2018.1412012

Bloom, P. J. (2003). *Leadership in action: How effective directors get things done.* Lake Forest, IL: New Horizons.

Bloom, P. J. (2007). *From the inside out: The power of reflection and self-awareness.* Lake Forest, IL: New Horizons.

Bloomberg, L. D. & Volpe, M. (2012). *Completing your qualitative dissertation: A road map from beginning to end.* Thousand Oaks: SAGE Publications, Inc.

Brindley, R., Fleege, P., & Graves, S. (2000). A friend in need: Mentorship and community. *Childhood Education, 76*(5), 312–316.

Brown, B. (2010). *The Gifts of Imperfection: Let Go of Who You Think You're Supposed to Be and Embrace Who You Are.* Center City: Hazelden.

Cameron, C., Mooney, A., Owen, C., & Moss, P. (2001). *Childcare students and nursery workers: Follow up surveys and in-depth interviews*, DfES Research Report 322.

CBC News (2022, January 19). B.C. early childhood educators say they're overworked, under-resourced and feeling ignored. https://www.cbc.ca/news/canada/british-columbia/bc-early-childhood-educators-covid-19-concerns-1.6321043

Chubbuck, S. M., Clift, R. T., Allard, J., & Quinlan, J. (2001). Playing it safe as a novice teacher: Implications for programs for new teachers. *Journal of Teacher Education, 52*(5), 365–376.

Correa, J. M., Martínez-Arbelaiz, A., & Aberasturi-Apraiz, E. (2015). Post-modern reality shock: Beginning teachers as sojourners in communities of practice. *Teaching and Teacher Education, 48*, 66–74. https://www.sciencedirect.com/science/article/abs/pii/S0742051X15000335?casa_token=iGTy1Ki8KfYAAAAA:a6-f9FdYPu1qK8bYV7-22naibvdOhFkn64Ss0hzI5Yj2IfQduWwapFBAAENePhbFl6La0GY

Costigliola, B. & Peek, S., Eds. (2009). A Bulletin of the Child Care Human Resource Sector Council. http://www.ccsc-cssge.ca/uploads/CCHRSspring09final.pdf

Creswell, J. W. & Plano Clark, V. L. (2007). *Designing and conducting mixed methods research.* Thousand Oaks: Sage Publications, Inc.

Denzin, N. K. & Lincoln, Y. S. (2005). *The sage handbook of qualitative research* (3rd ed.). Thousand Oaks: Sage Publications, Inc.

Department for Education (2017). Statutory framework for the early years foundation stage: Setting the standards for learning, development and care for children from birth to five. https://www.icmec.org/wp-content/uploads/2018/01/EYFS_STATUTORY_FRAMEWORK_2017.pdf

Department for Education (2021). Statutory Framework for the Early Years Foundation Stage: Setting the standards for learning, development and care for children from birth to five. https://assets.publishing.service.gov.uk/government/uploads/system/uploads/attachment_data/file/974907/EYFS_framework_-_March_2021.pdf

Devos, A. (2010). New teachers, mentoring and the discursive formation of professional identity. *Teaching and Teacher Education, 26*, 1219–1223.

Doan, L. K (2013). Mentoring needs of novice early childhood educators. *Canadian Children, 38*(2), 21–24. https://journals.uvic.ca/index.php/jcs/article/view/15447

Doan, L. K. (2014). *The early years: An exploration of the experiences and needs of novice early childhood educators in British Columbia* [Unpublished dissertation]. University of Calgary. https://prism.ucalgary.ca/handle/11023/1606

Doan, L. K. (2018). The power of connection: An induction support pilot project for ECEs in Kamloops. *The Early Childhood Educator, 32*(4), 14–15, 18. https://ecepeermentoring.trubox.ca/wp-content/uploads/sites/700/2021/01/The-Power-of-Connection-Article.pdf

Doan, L. K. (2019). Finding community: An exploration into an induction support pilot project. *Journal of Childhood Studies, 44*(1), 68–79. https://doi.org/10.18357/jcs.v44i1.18778

Doan, L. K. (2022). Peer mentoring communities of practice: A place to belong, ask questions, and grow. *The Early Childhood Educator, 37*(4), 16–18, 21.

Doan, L. K. & Gray, C. (2021). Mentoring as a strategy to address recruitment and retention in the early years sector. *The Early Childhood Educator, 36*(2), 20–25. https://ecepeermentoring.trubox.ca/wp-content/uploads/sites/700/2021/08/Mentorship-as-a-Strategy-to-Address-Recruitment-Doan-Gray-2021-2.pdf

Doan, L. K. & Jang, S. (2020). Peer mentoring project for early childhood educators in British Columbia [booklet].

Doan, L. K., Rawling, C., Mejia, N., Bailey, F., Lanphear, R., Kopetski, A., Robertson, A., & Schwartzentruber, H. (2021). Reflections on the province-wide peer mentoring project. *The Early Childhood Educator, 36*(1), 14–19.

Donegan, M. M., Ostrosky, M. M., & Fowler, S. A. (2000). Peer coaching: Teachers supporting teachers. *Young Children, 3*(9), 9–16.

Douglass, A. L. (2019). Leadership for quality early childhood education and care. OECD Education Working Paper No. 211. https://www.oecd.org/officialdocuments/publicdisplaydocumentpdf/?cote=EDU/WKP%282019%2919&docLanguage=En#page=1&zoom=auto,-197,848

DuFour, R. (2004). What is a "professional learning community"? *Educational Leadership, 61*(8), 6–11.

Early Childhood Educators of British Columbia (2009). I am an early childhood educator (Pamphlet).

Early Childhood Educators of British Columbia (2012). May 2012 is child care month: Early childhood educators matter to BC's economy (Media Release). http://www.ecebc.ca/news/ECEBC_ChildCareMonth_2012.pdf

Early Childhood Educators of British Columbia (2019). Community plan for a public system of integrated care and early learning. https://www.ecebc.ca/application/files/2115/7791/0563/0319_10aDay_Plan_8th_edition_web_Feb_27_2019_final.pdf

Early Childhood Educators of British Columbia (2022a). LOT program: Learning together outside. Early Childhood Educators of British Columbia. https://www.ecebc.ca/professional-development/lot-program

Early Childhood Educators of British Columbia (2022b). The role of the early childhood educator in British Columbia. https://www.ecebc.ca/application/files/5716/4617/5189/Position_Paper_-_The_Role_of_the_Early_Childhood_Educator_in_British_Columbia_rev.0226.pdf

Early Childhood Research and Development Team (2011). New Brunswick Curriculum Framework for Early Learning and Child Care. https://www2.gnb.ca/content/dam/gnb/Departments/ed/pdf/ELCC/ECHDPE/nb-curriculum-framework.pdf

Fantilli, R. D. & McDougall, D. E. (2009). A study of novice teachers: Challenges and supports in the first years. *Teaching and Teacher Education, 25*, 814–825.

Farewell, C. V., Quinlan, J., Melnick, E., Powers, J., & Puma, J. (2022). Job demands and resources experienced by the early childhood education workforce serving high-need populations. *Early Childhood Education Journal, 50*(2), 197–206. https://doi.org/10.1007/s10643-020-01143-4

Feiman-Nemser, S., Carver, C., Schwille, S., & Yusko, B. (1999). Beyond support: Taking new teachers seriously as learners. In M. Scherer (Ed.), *A better beginning: Supporting and mentoring new teachers* (pp. 3–12). Alexandria: Association for Supervision and Curriculum Development.

Finnish National Agency for Education (2022). National Core Curriculum for ECEC in a Nutshell. https://www.oph.fi/en/education-and-qualifications/national-core-curriculum-ecec-nutshell

Flanagan, K. (2011). PEI early learning framework: Relationships, environments, experiences. https://www.princeedwardisland.ca/sites/default/files/publications/eecd_eyfrwrk_full.pdf

Fleet, A. & Patterson, C. (2001). Professional growth reconceptualized: Early childhood staff searching for meaning. *Early Childhood Research and Practice, 3*(2). http://ecrp.uiuc.edu/v3n2/fleet.html

Flores, M. A. & Day, C. (2006). Contexts which shape and reshape new teachers' identities: A multi-perspective study. *Teaching and Teacher Education, 22*, 219–232.

Frede, E. C. (1995). The role of program quality in producing early childhood program benefits. *The Future of Children, 5*(3), 115–132.

Fresko, B. & Nasser-Abu Alhija, F. (2008). When intentions and reality clash: Inherent implantation difficulties of an induction program for new teachers. *Teaching and Teacher Education, 25*, 278–284.

Gamborg, L., Webb, A. W., Smith, A., & Baumgartner, J. J. (2018). Understanding self-efficacy of novice teachers during induction. *Research Issues in Contemporary Education, 3*(2), 16–26. https://files.eric.ed.gov/fulltext/EJ1244683.pdf

Gay, C. (2007). Developing a strategy for professional leaders. Early Childhood Educators of British Columbia Strategy Session. http://www.ecebc.ca/leadership/files/ECEBC_Strategy_Session.pdf

Gersten, R., Morvant, M., & Brengelman, S. (1995). Close to the classroom is close to the bone; Coaching as a means to translate research into practice. *Exceptional Children, 62*(1), 52–66.

Given, L. M. (2008). *The sage encyclopedia of qualitative research methods*. Los Angeles: Sage Publications.

Gold, Y. (1996). Beginning teacher support: Attrition, mentoring and induction. In J. Sikula, T. J. Buttery, & E. Guyton (Eds.), *Handbook of research on teacher education* (pp. 548–594). New York: Macmillan.

Government of Australia (2018). Belonging, being, and becoming: The early years learning framework for Australia. BELONGING, BEING & BECOMING (acecqa.gov.au)

Government of British Columbia (2019). British Columbia early learning framework. EarlyLearningFramework_2019_Web.pdf (mytrainingbc.ca).

Government of British Columbia (2022a). Early childhood educator certificate renewal form. https://www2.gov.bc.ca/assets/gov/education/early-learning/teach/ece/forms/renewal_ece_five_year_and_specializations_cf4104.pdf

Government of British Columbia (2022b). Early childhood profession in British Columbia. https://www2.gov.bc.ca/gov/content/education-training/early-learning/teach/training-and-professional-development/become-an-early-childhood-educator/ece-profession

Government of Ontario (2007). Early learning for every child today: A framework for Ontario early childhood settings. http://betterbeginningssudbury.ca/wp-content/uploads/2015/09/continuum.pdf

Government of Ontario (2013). Review of the early Childhood Educators Act, 2007 Consultation Report. http://www.edu.gov.on.ca/eng/new/2013/ECEAReviewReport.pdf

Grant, A. A., Jeon, L., & Buettner, C. K. (2019). Relating early childhood teachers' working conditions and well-being to their turnover intentions. *Educational Psychology, 39*(3), 294–312, doi: 10.1080/01443410.2018.1543856

Guba, E. G. & Lincoln, Y. S. (2005). Paradigmatic controversies, contradictions, and emerging confluences. In N. K. Denzin & Y. S. Lincoln (Eds.), *The sage handbook of qualitative research* (3rd ed., pp. 191–216). Thousand Oaks: Sage Publications, Inc.

Guervara, J. (2020). What does it mean to be an early childhood educator? Negotiating professionalism during practicum placements in Buenos Aires (Argentina). *European Early Childhood Education Research Journal, 28*(3), 439–449. http://doi.org/10.1080/1350293X.2020.1755500

Hargreaves, A. & Fullan, M. G. (1992). *Understanding teacher development*. New York: Teachers College Press.

Heidkmap, A. & Shapiro, J. (1999). The elements of a supportive induction program. In M. Scherer (Ed.), *A better beginning: Supporting and mentoring new teachers* (pp. 40–47). Alexandria: Association for Supervision and Curriculum Development.

Huston, T. & Weaver, C. L. (2008). Peer coaching: Professional development for experienced faculty. *Innovative Higher Education, 33*(1), 5–20.

Ingersoll, R. M. (2012). Beginning teacher induction: What the data tell us. *The Phi Delta Kappan*, 93(8), 47–51.

Jorde-Bloom, P. (1988). Factors influencing overall job satisfaction and organizational commitment in early childhood work environments. *Journal of Research in Childhood Education*, 3(2), 107–122.

Joyce, B. & Showers, B. (2002). Student achievement through staff development. In: B. Joyce & B. Showers, *Designing training and peer coaching: Our needs for learning*. Alexandria: ASCD. http://test.updc.org/assets/files/professional_development/umta/lf/randd-engaged-joyce.pdf

Joyce, B., Weil, M., & Showers, B. (1992). *Models of teaching*. Needham Heights: Simon & Schuster.

Joyce, B., Weil, M., & Showers, B. (1995). *Student achievement through staff development*. New York: Longman.

Katz, L. (1972). *Developmental stages of preschool teachers*. Urbana: Educational Resources Information Centre Clearinghouse on Early Childhood Education.

Kearney, S. P. (2011). The importance of induction programmes for beginning teachers in independent catholic secondary schools in New South Wales. Paper presented at the 9th Annual Hawaii International Conference on Education. Honolulu, Hawaii, 4–7 January.

Kernan, M., Casey, M., & Dowdall, M. (2022). Embracing changes outdoors for children under 3. In *30th European Early Childhood Education Research Association Conference Proceedings: Book of Abstracts*; August 23–26; Glasgow, Scotland. Abstract No. B 5. https://2022.eeceraconference.org/programme-outline/

Knoblock, N. A. & Whittington, M. S. (2002). Novice teachers' perceptions of support, teacher preparation quality, and student teaching experience related to teacher efficacy. *Journal of Vocational Education Research*, 27(3), 331–341.

Knowles, M. S., Holton, E. F., & Swanson, R. A. (2012). *The adult learner: The definitive classic in adult education and human resource development*. Abingdon: Routledge.

Kohler, F. W., McCullough, K. M., & Buchan, K. A. (1995). Using peer coaching to enhance preschool teachers' development and refinement of classroom activities. *Early Education & Development*, 6(3), 215–239.

Kristiansen, E., Tholin, K. R., & Bøe, M. (2021). Early childhood Centre directors coping with stress: Firefighters and oracles. *International Journal of Educational Management*. https://www.researchgate.net/profile/Kristin-Tholin/publication/350638772_Early_childhood_centre_directors_coping_with_stress_firefighters_and_oracles/links/615586e5ab3c1324134c9038/Early-childhood-centre-directors-coping-with-stress-firefighters-and-oracles.pdf

Kupila, P. & Karila, K. (2018). Peer mentoring as a support for beginning preschool teachers. *Professional Development in Education*, 45(2), 205–216. doi: 10.1080/19415257.2018.1427130

Kwon, K. A., Malek, A., Horm, D., & Castle, S. (2020). Turnover and retention of infant-toddler teachers: Reasons, consequences, and implications for practice and policy.

Children and Youth Services Review, 115, 105061. https://www.sciencedirect.com/sdfe/reader/pii/S019074091931504X/pdf

Langford, R. & Richardson, B. (2020). Ethics of care in practice: An observational study of interactions and power relations between children and educators in Urban Ontario early childhood settings. *Journal of Childhood Studies, 45*(1), 33–47. https://doi.org/10.18357/jcs00019398

Lave, J. & Wenger, E. (1991). *Situated learning: Legitimate peripheral participation.* New York: Cambridge University Press.

Lave, J. & Wenger, E. (1998). *Communities of practice: Learning, meaning, and identity.* Cambridge: Cambridge University Press.

Long, H. B. (2004). Understanding adult learners. In M. W. Galbraith (Ed.), *Adult learning methods: A guide for effective instruction* (3rd ed.). Florida: Krieger Publishing.

Long, S. (1997). Separating rhetoric from reality: Supporting teachers in negotiating beyond the status quo. *Journal of Teacher Education, 55*(2), 141–153.

Luft, J. A., Roehrig, G. H., & Patterson, N. C. (2002). Barriers and pathways: A reflection on the implementation of an induction program for secondary science teachers. *School Science and Mathematics, 102*(5), 222–228.

Lynch, R. G. & Vaghul, K. (2015). The benefits and costs of investing in early childhood education: The fiscal, economic, and societal gains of a universal prekindergarten program in the United States, 2016–2050. Washington Center for Equitable Growth. http://cdn.equitablegrowth.org/wp-content/uploads/2015/12/02110123/early-childhood-ed-report-web.pdf

Magill, A. L. (2002). *Studying the needs and experiences of beginning teachers* [Unpublished masters thesis]. Alberta: University of Alberta.

Mahmood, S. (2013). "Reality shock": New early childhood education teachers. *Journal of Early Childhood Teacher Education, 34*, 154–170. https://www.tandfonline.com/doi/abs/10.1080/10901027.2013.787477

Makovichuk, L., Hewes, J., Lirette, P., & Thomas, N. (2014). Flight: Alberta's early learning and care framework. Flight Framework Document F.pdf

Manlove, E. E. (1993). Multiple correlates of burnout in child care workers. *Early Childhood Research Quarterly, 8*(4), 499–518.

Mary Immaculate College (2022). Professional Mentoring in Early Childhood Practice. Faculty of Education. https://www.mic.ul.ie/faculty-of-education/programme/professional-mentoring-in-early-childhood-practice

Mayfield, M. I. (2001). *Early childhood education and care in Canada: Contexts, dimensions, and issues.* Toronto: Pearson Education.

McCuaig, K., Akbari, E., & Correia, A. (2022). Canada's children need a professional early childhood education workforce. Atkinson Center for Society and Child Development, Ontario Institute for Studies in Education, University of Toronto. https://ecereport.ca/en/workforce-report/

McDonald, P., Thorpe, K., & Irvine, S. (2018a). Low pay but still we stay: Retention in early childhood education and care. *Journal of Industrial Relations*, *60*(5), 647–668. https://doi.org/10.1177/0022185618800351

McMullen, M. B., Lee, M. S., McCormick, K. I., & Choi, J. (2020). Early childhood professional well-being as a predictor of the risk of turnover in childcare: A matter of quality. *Journal of Research in Childhood Education*, *34*(3), 331–345. https://www.researchgate.net/profile/Mary-Mcmullen/publication/338956362_Early_Childhood_Professional_Well-Being_as_a_Predictor_of_the_Risk_of_Turnover_in_Child_Care_A_Matter_of_Quality/links/5fc148eda6fdcc6cc676530b/Early-Childhood-Professional-Well-Being-as-a-Predictor-of-the-Risk-of-Turnover-in-Child-Care-A-Matter-of-Quality.pdf

Meristo, M. & Eisenschmidt, E. (2014). Novice teachers' perceptions of school climate and self-efficacy. *International Journal of Educational Research*, *67*, 1–19. https://doi.org/10.1016/j.ijer.2014.04.003

Miles, M. B., Huberman, A. M., & Saldana, J. (2014). *Qualitative data analysis: A methods sourcebook* (3rd ed.). Thousand Oaks: SAGE Publications, Inc.

Moloney, M. (2010). Professional identity in early childhood care and education: Perspectives of pre-school and infant teachers. *Irish Educational Studies*, *29*(2), 167–187.

Moore, A. & Towler, M. (2022). The fusion of theory and practice: Reflection on the early years & childhood studies professional practice placement through a community of practice (CoP) experience. In *30th European Early Childhood Education Research Association Conference Proceedings: Book of Abstracts*; August 23–26; Glasgow, Scotland. Abstract nr A 10. https://2022.eeceraconference.org/programme-outline/

Murray, J. (2006). Designing and implementing a mentoring scheme: University of Worcester surestart-recognized sector-endorsed foundation degree in early years. In A. Robins (Ed.), *Mentoring in the early years* (pp. 63–78). London: Paul Chapman Publishing.

National Council for Curriculum and Assessment (2009). Aistear: The early childhood curriculum framework. http://www.ibe.unesco.org/fileadmin/user_upload/archive/curricula/ireland/ie_ece_fw_2009_eng.pdf

Neuman, M. J., Josephson, K., & Chua, P. G. (2015). A Review of the literature: Early childhood care and education (ECCE) personnel in low- and middle-income countries. https://unesdoc.unesco.org/ark:/48223/pf0000234988

New Zealand Government (2017). Te Whāriki He whāriki mātauranga mō ngā mokopuna o Aotearoa Early childhood curriculum. https://www.education.govt.nz/assets/Documents/Early-Childhood/ELS-Te-Whariki-Early-Childhood-Curriculum-ENG-Web.pdf

Nicholson, S. & Reifel, S. (2011). Sink or swim: Child care teachers' perceptions of entry training experiences. *Journal of Childhood Teacher Education*, *32*(1), 5–25. https://eric.ed.gov/?id=EJ915968

Noble, K. & Macfarlane, K. (2005). Romance or reality?: Examining burnout in early childhood teachers. *Australian Journal of Early Childhood, 30*(3), 53–58.

OECD (n.d.). Encouraging Quality in Early Childhood Education and Care. Research Brief: Working Conditions Matter. https://www.oecd.org/education/school/49322250.pdf

OECD (2005). *Teachers matter: Attracting, developing and retaining effective teachers.* Paris: Author.

Ontario College of Teachers (2006). *New teacher induction: Growing the profession.* Toronto: Author.

Ozgun, O. (2005). *The relationship of novice Turkish early childhood education teachers' professional needs, experiences, efficacy beliefs, school climate for promoting early childhood learning, and job satisfaction* [Unpublished doctoral dissertation]. New York: Syracuse University.

Peterson Miller, S., Harris, C., & Watanabe, A. (1991). Professional coaching: A method for increasing effective and decreasing ineffective teacher behaviours. *Teacher Education and Special Education: The Journal of the Teacher Education Division of the Council for Exceptional Children, 14*(3), 183–191.

Piggot-Irvine, E., Aitken, H., Ritchie, J., Ferguson, P., & McGrath, P. (2009). Induction of newly qualified teachers in New Zealand. *Asia-Pacific Journal of Teacher Education, 37*(2), 175–198, doi: 10.1080/13598660902804030

Poulter Jewson, B. (2020). Coaching teams of early years professionals throughout a county in England. In M. Gasper & R. Walker (Eds.), *Mentoring and coaching in early childhood education* (pp. 135–144). London: Bloomsbury Academic.

Recchia, S. L. & Puig, V. I. (2019). Early childhood teachers finding voice among peers: A reflection on practice. *The New Educator, 15*(1), 51–65.

Roach O'Keefe, A., Hooper, S., & Jakubiec, B. (2019). Exploring early childhood educators' notions about professionalism in Prince Edward Island. *Journal of Childhood Studies, 44*(1), 20–36.

Robertson, H. J. (1992). Teacher development and gender equity. In A. Hargreaves & M. G. Fullan (Eds.), *Understanding Teacher Development* (pp. 43–61). New York: Teachers College Press.

Rodd, J. (2006). *Leadership in early childhood* (3rd ed.). New York: Open University Press.

Rodd, J. (2013). *Leadership in early childhood* (4th ed.). New York: Open University Press.

Rolfe, H. (2005). Building a stable workforce: Recruitment and retention in the child care and early years sector. *Children & Society, 19*, 55–65.

Sabar, N. (2004). From heaven to reality through crisis: Novice teachers as migrants. *Teaching and Teacher Education, 20*, 145–161.

Sachs, J. (2000). The activist professional. *Journal of Educational Change, 1*, 77–95.

Salminen, J. (2017). Early Childhood Education and Care System in Finland. https://www.semanticscholar.org/paper/Early-Childhood-Education-and-Care-System-in-Salminen/9f6649eb70d354027d4ed8b494126bcd96832f6f

Senge, P. (2022). https://conversational-leadership.net/quotation/quote-sharing-knowledge-not-same-as-information-sharing/

Showers, B. (1984). *Peer coaching: A strategy for facilitating transfer of training*. Eugene: Center for Educational Policy and Management.

Showers, B. (1985). Teachers coaching teachers: Schools restructured to support the development of peer coaching teams create norms of collegiality and experimentation. *Educational Leadership*, 42(7), 43–49.

Showers, B. & Joyce, B. (1996). The evolution of peer coaching. *Educational Leadership*, 53(6), 12–16.

Skaalvik, E. M. & Skaalvik, S. (2009). Teacher self-efficacy and teacher burnout: A study of relations. *Teaching and Teacher Education*, 26, 1059–1069.

Snider, K. & Holley, M. (2020). Using collaborative coaching when teachers are experts. In M. Gasper & R. Walker (Eds.), *Mentoring and coaching in early childhood education* (pp. 135–144). London: Bloomsbury Academic.

Social Research and Demonstration Corporation (2021). Evaluation of Early Care and Learning Recruitment and Retention Strategy: Evaluation Report 2020. https://www.ecebc.ca/application/files/3116/2326/4444/Evaluation_Report_2020_Deliverable_15_04Jun2021.pdf

Sparks, G. M. & Bruder, S. (1987). Before and after peer coaching. *Educational Leadership*, 45(3), 54–57.

Taylor-Leonhardi, M. (2022). Personal Communication.

Thornton, K., Wansbrough, D., Clarkin-Phillips, J., Aitken, H., & Tamati, A. (2009). *Conceptualizing leadership in early childhood education in Aotearoa New Zealand*. New Zealand: New Zealand Teachers Council.

Totenhagen, C. J., Hawkins, S. A., Casper, D. M., & Bosch, L. A. (2016). Retaining early childhood education workers: A review of the empirical literature. *Journal of Research in Childhood Education*, 30(4), 585–599.

Tschannen-Moran, M., Woolfolk Hoy, A., & Hoy, W. K. (1998). Teacher efficacy: Its meaning and measure. *Review of Educational Research*, 68, 202–248.

Tschantz, J. M. & Vail, C. O. (2000). Effects of peer coaching on the rate of responsive teacher statements during a child-directed period in an inclusive preschool setting. *Teacher Education and Special Education: The Journal of the Teacher Education Division of the Council for Exceptional Children*, 23(3), 189–201.

UNESCO (2022). Early childhood care and education: An investment in wellbeing, gender equality, and social cohesion. https://www.unesco.org/en/education/early-childhood

United Kingdom Government (2021). Statutory framework for the early years foundation stage: Setting the standards for learning, development and care for children from birth to five. Statutory framework for the early years foundation stage (publishing.service.gov.uk).

Vander Ven, K. (1988). Pathways to professional effectiveness for early childhood educators. In B. Spodek, O. Saracho, & D. Peters (Eds.) *Professionalism and the early childhood practitioner* (pp. 137–160). New York: Teachers College Press.

Veenman, S. (1984). Perceived problems of beginning teachers. *Review of Educational Research*, 54(2), 143–178.

Viotti, S., Guidetti, G., Sottimano, I., Martini, M., & Converso, D. (2019). Work ability and burnout: What comes first? *A two-wave, cross-lagged study among early childhood educators. Safety Science, 118*, 898–906. https://reader.elsevier.com/reader/sd/pii/S0925753518315558?token=0A3C2ABD4AB4331FAD814F68E9A448F675E9B4C1EA651EACDB438A60846C264C1BC4F569CCB587DA2A585DC2F8F33671&originRegion=us-east-1&originCreation=20220323190131

Vygotsky, L. (1986). *Thought and language.* United States of America: The Massachusetts Institute of Technology.

Weasmer, J. & Woods, A. M. (2003). Mentoring: Professional development through reflection. *The Teacher Educator, 39*(1), 64–77.

Weaver, P. E. (2004). The culture of teaching and mentoring compliance. *Childhood Education 80*(5), 258–260.

Wenger, E. (1998). *Communities of practice: Learning, meaning, and identity.* New York: Cambridge University Press.

Wenger, E. (2000). Communities of practice and social learning systems. *Organization, 7*(2), 225–246.

Wenger, E., McDermott, R., & Snyder, W. M. (2002). *Cultivating communities of practice.* Boston: Harvard Business School Publishing.

Wenger, E. C. & Snyder, W. M. (2000). Communities of practice: The organisational frontier. *Harvard Business Review, 78*(1), 139–146.

Whatman, J. (2016). *Supporting a system-wide shift from advice and guidance to educative mentoring.* Wellington: New Zealand Council for Educational Research. https://www.nzcer.org.nz/system/files/Supporting%20a%20system-wide%20shift%20from%20advice%20and%20guidance%20to%20educative%20mentoring.pdf

Whitebrook, M. & Sakai, L. (1995). *The potential of mentoring: An assessment of the California early childhood mentor teacher program.* Washington, DC: National Center for the Early Childhood Work Force.

Whitebrook, M. & Sakai, L. (2003). Turnover begets turnover: An examination of job and occupational instability among child care centre staff. *Early Childhood Research Quarterly, 18*(3), 273–293.

Winstead Fry, S. (2010). The analysis of an unsuccessful novice teacher's induction experiences: A case study presented through layered account. *The Qualitative Report, 15*(5), 1164–1190.

Wlodkowski, R. J. (2004). Strategies to enhance adult motivation to learn. In M. W. Galbraith (Ed.), *Adult learning methods: A guide for effective instruction* (3rd ed., pp. 91–112). Florida: Krieger Publishing.

Wood, K. C., Smith, H., & Grossniklaus, D. (2001). Piaget's stages of cognitive development. In M. Orey (Ed.), *Emerging perspectives on learning, teaching, and technology.* Retrieved December 9, 2012 from http://projects.coe.uga.edu/epltt/

Zepeda, S. J. (2012). *Professional development: What works* (2nd ed.). Larchmont: Eye on Education, Inc.

Index

administrative practices
    adjustment to   72–3
    questionnaire, closed and open-ended   19
adult learning theory (theory of andragogy)   15, 22, 30–1, 41, 99, 133
    andragogik   30
    andragogy and pedagogy   30–1
    attitude   32–3
    critical questioning and predicting   33
    description   15
    experiences of the learner   103–4
    learning situations   103
    motivation   31–2
    professional development   135
    purpose within learning experience   33
Aitken, H.   12, 123
Association of Early Childhood Educators of Ontario (AECEO)   139
Australia
    early learning frameworks   3–5
    high job satisfaction, findings of   96

Bachelor of Early Childhood Education   12
Bandura, A.   15, 28–9, 102
Beaton, L.   140
best practice for early childhood educators
    British Columbia, induction support   110
    communities of practice   123
    constructive feedback   110
    data   123–4
    Doan model (*see* Doan model of best practice for the induction)
    ECEBC, accreditation process   122
    government policy   122
    implications   119–21
    induction-related activities   110
    limitations   123–4
    longevity of different groups   121
    new knowledge (*see* new knowledge, introduction of)
    post-secondary institutions   122–3
    professional development opportunities   120–1
    research   121–3
    theory of educator development   124
British Columbia, induction support in
    barriers   102
    colleague at work, support from   102
    communication   101
    critical peers instead of mentors   103
    educators as paid or volunteer work in a licensed program   2
    experienced *vs.* new educator   99
    findings, qualitative and quantitative data   105
    identity, crisis of   102–4
    innovative work, lack of support for   98
    lack of supervisory visits to the classroom   101
    learning and reality of the classroom   102
    level of teacher efficacy   99
    mentoring   98, 100
    "one-size-fits-all" approach   98
    passion, lack of   99
    Peer Mentoring Program for Early Childhood Educators in   140–1
    practical and theoretical implications   103–5
    prior experiences, value for   99
    professional association   104–5
    repetitious meetings   98
    services of ECEBC   101
    shortage of educators   9
    specific induction needs   97
    theory of zones of proximal development, Vygotsky's   104

time period 97
working environment 8–9
workplace as learning environment 104
British Columbia Aboriginal Child Care Society (BCACCS) 138

Cameron, C. 96, 100–1
campus-based child care 8
Canada
   AECEO, Ontario 139
   educators, registered as assistants or as certified 2
   imposter syndrome 132
   lack of structure to support educators 7
   Peer Mentoring Program, Ontario 139
Child Care Human Resources Sector Council 9
Chua, P. G. 2, 96, 125
Chubbuck, S. M. 97
coaching 36–9
   expert coaching 36
   peer coaching (*see* peer coaching)
   reciprocal coaching 36
College of Early Childhood Educators of Ontario 102
communities of practice 142
   benefits 35
   hands-on participation 33–6
   improving schools, goal of 35
   learning goals, work towards 35
   learning within 33–6
   managers, support from 34
   model for research 133–5
   participation in a community of practice, significance of 33
   and professional learning communities 36–7
   time spent within the peer-mentoring 134
Community Plan for a Public System of Integrated Early Care and Learning (ECEBC, 2019) 12

Day, C. 102
Denzin, N. K. 18
Developing a Strategy for Professional Leadership (report) 27
Doan model of best practice for the induction 118–19
Dufour, R. 35

Early Childhood Education and Care (ECE or ECEC)
early childhood education program,
   adjustment to 45–7
   adjustment to new role 47–9
   being a mentor 56–7
   building relationships 52
   connection with experienced educator 46
   good team 50
   good working environment 52
   interviews, findings
      lack of communication 60
      pedagogical narration 59
      philosophical differences, issue of 57–60, 96
      preparedness 57–8
      supervisor, issue of 60
   negative experiences 51
   open-ended question 48–9
   personal qualities 54
   post-secondary system in British Columbia 47
   preservice personal experiences 53–4
   preservice professional experiences 50
   professional development 52–3, 56
   question related to support 45–6, 48
   quotes, from survey 47
   role model or mentor 53
   support
      from administrators or supervisors 54–5
      from family and/or friends 53
      staff 56
   teamwork 55
   themes 49, 54
   work experiences 51–2
early childhood educators, development of
   adult learning theory (theory of andragogy) 30–3
   coaching 36–9

difficulty in connecting theory to practice   11–12
educators experience and effects on children   10
instructor and sponsor educator   7
leadership in   8, 10, 12
learning within communities of practice   33–6
mentoring   7, 12, 39–41
motivation of adult learners to learn   32–3
professional identity development   26–8
programs within post-secondary institutions   7
qualifications   2
quality of   1, 11
research question   10
support in their first year of work   11
teacher efficacy   28–30
terms and definitions   3–6
Early Childhood Educators of British Columbia (ECEBC)   12, 24, 138
The Early Learning Framework   59
Elliot, Enid   138
Erasmus Foundation   140
expert coaching   36, 39

family resource centers   9
Fantilli, R. D.   98
field of early childhood education, adjusting to   64–5
  challenges   66–7
  classroom, adjustment to   62–4
  job satisfaction   68–9
  open-ended question   65–6
  perceived needs   64
  positive aspects of   67
  strategies and approaches   69
  survey   62–4
Fleet, A.   28
Flores, M. A.   102
Fresko, B.   99

Gay, C.   98

head start programs   9
Henderson, Elizabeth   140
Hendra, Karolyn   138

Holton, E. F.   30–2, 104
identity development, professional   26–8
  consolidation, stage of   27
  induction activities   27
  maturity, stage of   26
  mentor's assistance   26
  model of educator development   26
  renewal, stage of   26
  stages of educator development, Katz's   26–7, 95
  stages of professionalism, Vander Ven's   27–8
  survival, stage of   26
  teacher training *vs.* classroom reality   26
  young age of educators   26
imposter syndrome   132
Indigenous Elders   138
induction support, interview survey
  context for   85
  findings   90–1
  ideal induction program   93
  induction-related activities   85, 89
  introduction of educators   91–2
  mentoring   90–1
  percentage of received activities   88
  professional development   92
  questionnaire data   85, 89
  rank order of scales based on level of need   89
  standards in place for activities   94
  support
    from early childhood education community   93–4
    for new educators   90–2
    percentage of support received   86–7
  supportive work environment   92–3
  what was not received   89
Induction Support Pilot Project   125
infant-toddler child care   8
Ingersoll, R. M.   96, 98
Ireland
  community of practice model   140
  educators, perceived to be "just the babysitter"   102
  Level 8 Special Purpose Certificate   139
Irvine, S.   96

job satisfaction   23, 68–9, 95–7
   adjusting to the field of early education (*see* field of early childhood education, adjusting to)
   descriptive statistics for measuring   21
   and teacher efficacy   29
Jorde-Bloom, P.   95–6
Josephson, K.   96
Joyce, B.   37

Kapp, Alexander   30
Katz, L.   9, 13, 15, 26–7, 95, 109, 115–7, 124
Knoblock, N. A.   29
Knowles, M. S.   15, 30–2, 99, 103–4, 133, 135

laboratory/demonstration nursery schools   9
Lave, J.   15, 33, 103–4, 116, 124
Learning On the Land Together (LOT)   138
Life preserver   143
Lincoln, Y. S.   18
Long, H. B.   32, 99
Luft, J. A.   102

McDermott, R.   133
McDonald, P.   96
McDougall, D. E.   98
Magill, A. L.   18
mentoring   39–41
   benefits of   39
   connect with an experienced practitioner   39
   culture of learning   39
   for first year of teaching   12
   obstacles
      lack of up-to-date information on innovations   40
      little time for collaborative planning   40
      power difference   40–1
      professional growth   40
      support in the workplace   39
Moloney, Mary   139
Mooney, A.   101
Moore, Alison   139

Moss, P.   101
motivation   31–2
   of adult learners   32–3
   collaborative learning   33
   critical questioning and predicting   33
   description   32
   goals and assessment   33

Nasser-Abu Alhija, F.   98–9
new knowledge, introduction of   110–24
   educators, treatment of   113
   isolated ECE workplace   115, 116
   jobsite as a community of practice   114, 117
   models of perception (*see* perception, models of)
   need for instruction   116
   needs of educators in the survival year   117
   regular, daily communication with colleagues   115
   stages, developmental model   115
   support from peers and co-workers   115, 117
New Zealand
   longer training time   98
   mentor, role of   7, 12, 27
   teacher induction, study on   13
   teacher registration process, fear about   123
   two- to five-year process of induction and support   2
Nicholson, S.   34, 96, 101–2

OECD   13, 27, 95, 100
open-ended questionnaire   19, 23, 48–9, 54, 64–6, 73
Owen, C.   101
Ozgun, O.   18, 96

parental engagements   140
parent cooperative nursery schools   8, 9
Patterson, N. C.   28, 102
pedagogical narrations (PNs)   59, 98, 131–3, 138
peer coaching   36, *see also* peer mentoring
   benefits   37
   challenges and barriers   38–9

collaborative process 37
feedback and/or critique 37
latest technologies 37
nonthreatening approach with a
    peer 38
power differences 38
sense of collegiality 37
training sessions on specific teaching
    skills and strategies 37
peer mentoring 130, *see also* programs
    of support
  benefits of 13, 127–8
  community of practice 128, 142, 144
  Early Learning and Child Care
    Legislation in BC 134
  ECEBC Code of Ethics 134
  Educator Health and Well-being 134
  Indigenous Perspectives and
    Worldviews 134
  Peer Mentoring Project 126
  prepared environment, impact
    of 127–8
  program 24–5
  Reflective Practice 134
Peer Mentoring Program, Ontario 139
perception, models of
  educators, how they want to be
    treated 112, 113
  feedback, informal and/or
    formal 114
  interest towards new educators
    113–14
  learn the reality 112
  left alone, feeling of 111
  model of how new educators are
    perceived 111
  team work 114
  value for the work 112
Piaget, J. 28
play therapy programs 9
professional capacity, development of
  career in future 83–4
  community experiences 82
  induction activities 80
  interview, findings from 74–84
  preservice experiences 82
  support
    from coworkers 83
    from friends 78

inconsistent induction 79–80
inconsistent level of 74–6
informal mentoring 80
  from jobsite 76–8
lack of 74–6
mentor 80
  from post-secondary
    instructors 78
supervisor's feedback 79
workplace 81
programs of support 125–7, *see also* peer
    mentoring
  autonomy, peer mentoring
    communities 126–7
  desire for an induction program 125
  Peer Mentoring Project 126
  setting up of
    confidentiality 129–30
    listen to the educators 129
    mentor-mentee or mentor-protégé
      model 132
    non-hierarchical approach 131
    pedagogical narrations (PNs) 59,
      98, 131–3, 138
    research-informed background
      for 131–3
  successful Peer Mentoring
    Program 130
Provisionally Registered Teachers 13

reciprocal coaching 36
Reifel, S. 34, 96
research
  adult learning theory, Knowles' 15
  Child Care Resource and Referral
    Programs 135
  collaborative research 14
  community of practice theory 15
  constructivist perspective 136–7
  data analysis 19–20
  descriptive statistics on six scale 20
  educators' experiences and needs
    14–15
  focus on leadership in ECE 13
  implications for 13–14
  interviews, results from 21
  methods
    data collection 18
    five-point Likert scale 19

online questionnaire 19
open-ended questions 19
research ethics 18
sampling 18
survey and interviews 17
multiple ways to participate 136–7
need for ongoing programs of
 support 128–9
participants, demographic
 characteristics 16–17
participatory research 14
partnerships 135
peer-mentoring community of practice
 (*see* peer mentoring)
professional identity development 15
programs of support (*see* programs of
 support)
pseudonyms 19–20
qualitative researchers 136
questions 16, 21–2
sharing presentation and/or
 workshop 135–6
teacher efficacy 15
theoretical framework 13–14
using the community of practice model
 (*see* communities of practice)
wages, raise in 137–8
Rodd, J. 13–14, 39
Roehrig, G. H. 102
Rolfe, H. 101

Sachs, J. 104–5
Sakai, L. 28
Savicevic, Dusan 30
school-age child care 8
Scotland
 emphasis on learning outdoors
  140
 power of communities of practice and
  peer mentoring 141
Showers, B. 37
Skaalvik, S. 29
Snyder, W. M. 33–4, 133
social learning theory, Vygotsky's 30
Strong Start programs 8–9
supervisory practices, adjustment to
 administrative practices 72–3
 communication, importance of
  71

constructive criticism 72
context for 70
interviews, findings from (*see*
 professional capacity,
 development of)
open-ended questions on feedback,
 skills and time 73–4
primary supervisor, help from 71
regular meeting 72
support 70–1
Swanson, R. A. 30–2, 104

teacher efficacy 28–9
 burnout symptoms of teachers 29
 collective efficacy of the teaching
  team 29–30
 definition 28
 development of 29–30
 factors influencing efficacy 30
 positive feedback, support,
  guidance 29
 self-efficacy 28
 social cognitive theory, Bandura's
  28
teen-parent programs 9
theory of zones of proximal development,
 Vygotsky's 104
Thompson Rivers University Research
 Ethics Board 18
Thornton, K. 13
Thorpe, K. 96
Towler, Marcella 139

United Kingdom
 early learning framework 5
 high job satisfaction, findings of
  26
 young age, childcare students and
  staff 26
United States
 ECPMG, created to support
  educators 7
 report of work satisfaction 96
University of Cork 139
University of Worcester 39

Vander Ven, K. 15, 27
Veenman, S. 26–7
Vygotsky, L. 30, 104

Wenger, E. 15, 33–5, 103, 104, 116, 124, 133
Whitebrook, M. 28
Whittingdon, M. S. 29
Winstead Fry, S. 98
Wlodkowski, R. J. 32–3
work environment
   campus-based child care 8
   family resource centers 9
   head start programs 9
   high turnover of staff 9
   infant-toddler child care 8
   issues within the work environment 8
   laboratory/demonstration nursery schools 9
   need for additional training 9–10
   parent cooperative nursery schools 8, 9
   play therapy programs 9
   school-age child care 8
   shortage of early childhood educators 9
   strong Start programs 8
   teen-parent programs 9
workload 20, 30, 57–8, 64, 95–7, 101

www.ingramcontent.com/pod-product-compliance
Lightning Source LLC
Chambersburg PA
CBHW052127300426
44116CB00010B/1809